PENGUIN BOOKS

T0342583

Three plays

Novels
An Open Swimmer
Shallows
That Eye, the Sky
In the Winter Dark
Cloudstreet
The Riders
Dirt Music
Breath
Eyrie
The Shepherd's Hut

Stories
Scission
Minimum of Two
The Turning

For Younger Readers
Jesse
Lockie Leonard, Human Torpedo
The Bugalugs Bum Thief
Lockie Leonard, Scumbuster
Lockie Leonard, Legend
Blueback
The Deep

Non-fiction
Land's Edge
Local Colour (with Bill Bachman)
Down to Earth (with Richard Woldendorp)
Smalltown (with Martin Mischkulnig)
Island Home
The Boy Behind the Curtain

Plays
Rising Water
Signs of Life
Shrine

TIM WINTON

Three plays

PENGUIN BOOKS

PENGUIN BOOKS

Penguin Books is part of the Penguin Random House group of companies,
whose addresses can be found at global.penguinrandomhouse.com.

Rising Water first published by Currency Press Pty Ltd, 2012
Signs of Life first published by Penguin Group (Australia), 2013
Shrine first published by Penguin Group (Australia), 2014
This collected edition published by Penguin Random House Australia Pty Ltd, 2022

Cover design by Design by Committee © Penguin Random House Australia Pty Ltd
Cover photograph © Trent Parke / Snapper Media
Text design by Samantha Jayaweera © Penguin Random House Australia Pty Ltd
Typeset in Garamond by Midland Typesetters (*Rising Water*), Penguin Random House
Australia Pty Ltd (*Signs of Life*) and Post Pre-Press Group (*Shrine*)
Printed and bound in Australia by Griffin Press, an accredited
ISO AS/NZS 14001 Environmental Management Systems printer

Director's notes © Kate Cherry, 2012–14. Production notes adapted
from the programs of the Black Swan Theatre Company.
Production photography by Gary Marsh and courtesy Black Swan Theatre Company, except
for: pages 156 and 259 photos by Robert Frith, page 261 poster reproduced courtesy of
Sydney Theatre Company and photo by Grant Sparkes-Carroll, pages 262–265 photos by
Garry Ferguson, and page 266 photo by Lisa Tomasetti, courtesy of Sydney Theatre Company.

 A catalogue record for this
book is available from the
National Library of Australia

ISBN 978 1 76104 531 8

penguin.com.au

FOR KATE CHERRY

Contents

Rising Water

Contents

From left: Col (Geoff Kelso) and Baxter (John Howard)

A marina in Fremantle in Western Australia on the evening of Australia Day.

CHARACTERS

COL	a man in his early 60s, owner and resident of the yacht *Goodness*
BAXTER	a man in his 50s, owner and resident of the yacht *Shirley*
JACKIE	a woman in her late 40s, owner and resident of the sloop *Mercy*
DEE	an English tourist in her early 20s
PASSERBY	
BOY	
DRUNKEN BOOFHEAD	
SKIPPER	
RAY	a boatie
REVELLER	
SEAGOING GENTLEMAN	

Jackie (Alison Whyte)

Jackie (Alison Whyte) and Baxter (John Howard)

Col (Geoff Kelso) and Baxter (John Howard)

ACT I

Howling wind. The groan of mooring ropes and the whine and clank of rigging until the breeze gives out and a magical calm ensues in which there is only the lapping of water.

Light up on:

A wooden jetty at sunset. From a boardwalk at stage left, the jetty juts westward into the still water of a marina. Three boats, the old sloop Mercy, *a ragged little sailboat* Shirley, *and the much sleeker ocean-going yacht* Goodness, *lie moored in a row from stage left. The stepped mast of the westernmost boat, the* Goodness, *sprawls across the jetty at stage right. It's the only vessel moored sternwards to the jetty. Sounds of the city at day's end: traffic, car alarms, sirens, snatches of music, bird cries. The shadow of a seabird plays across the water and as it tracks westward a* BOY *appears rowing a dinghy languidly. At stage left he pauses to watch the sinuous dance of the bird shadow*

9

flowing across masts, boats, piles, ropes. As it plays across his face he is enchanted, transfixed. The everyday sounds of the marina fall away. The bird shadow encroaches slowly to obscure the BOY's face and then the light around him breaks up and fades until he disappears altogether. Silence is broken by the splash of a jumping fish.

Light on the Shirley *as* BAXTER *pokes his head up in the companionway, alerted to the presence of something he can't see. He sits on deck. The ambient noise of the marina returns.*

A car engine idles. A car door slams and a vehicle pulls away as JACKIE *enters in a business suit, wheeling cabin luggage down the boardwalk and then onto the jetty, unaware she's being watched. At the* Mercy *she kicks off her shoes and drops them aboard, takes up suitcase, briefcase, handbag and boards, checking on the state of the boat as she unlocks and goes below. Her cabin light comes on. She cracks a hatch, undresses, comes back on deck in shorts and t-shirt with her jacket on a hanger, which she hooks to the boom for airing.* JACKIE *sucks in a lungful of air, pulls her hair free, yawns and goes below for bed, drawing a sarong across the open hatch in readiness for sleep.*

COL enters, in shorts, singlet and ancient tennis shoes. Singing a patriotic jingle, he lurches drunkenly down the boardwalk with a carton of beer on his shoulder and a string bag of cauliflowers swinging from his free hand.

> COL: [*singing*] Someday we'll all be together once
> more . . .

As he draws alongside the middle boat, Shirley, *a bedraggled yacht, the shadow of a bird passes over him.*

And all of the ships come back to the—

BAXTER *observes for a moment, and then, as if to distract himself, he takes up a rope tied to his safety rail. Above him in the rigging hangs a melange of salvaged junk, a pram, a stop sign, a bike. From the water he hauls up a crab net.*

So ends another day in paradise.

    BAXTER: [*muttering*] Paradise, purgatory. Whatever you reckon, Col.

As BAXTER *shakes a crab into a steel bucket,* COL *gives up on the singlet and kicks off his tennis shoes. Without a free hand he has a little trouble getting himself aboard his vessel. After his second attempt he notices* BAXTER *watching, amused.*

    COL: You could offer to give a man a hand.

    BAXTER: Didn't like to overstep—

    COL: Oh, bugger it.

COL *heaves the box of beer aboard with a thud.*

    BAXTER: [*gesturing toward* JACKIE'*s boat, indicating that she's asleep*] Hey, steady on.

COL: She'd sleep through sex with George Clooney.

BAXTER: Even so.

COL: [*attempting to lower his voice*] When she get in?

BAXTER: This arvo.

COL *swings down as* BAXTER *proffers a fresh crab by way of conciliation, but* COL *waves him away.*

COL: Told you before, ya wood duck. Keep eatin
    those buggers you'll end up glowin in the dark.

BAXTER: Anything to be noticed, Col.

COL: My arse. Never seen a man lying lower. A crab
    is a scum-suckin bottom feeder.

BAXTER: As ever, Col, you are a font of marine
    wisdom.

COL: You got any idea what settles on the seabed
    here?

BAXTER: Yeah, well I'm not entirely stupid.

COL: The effluvium of a hundred thousand bilges.

BAXTER: Effluvium?

COL: Every blind mullet and slow-sinkin Chokito.
Two centuries of shit, son.

BAXTER: Honestly, I don't think—

COL: Cancerous chemicals! Toxic smegma!

BAXTER: Hey, Skip, you're talking about my dinner.

COL *takes a few six packs below and calls up.*

COL: [*from below*] The crab, my son—

He pops back up.

—the crab is the ocean's welfare cheat!

COL *goes below again and* BAXTER *addresses the offending crustacean.*

BAXTER: You benthic bludger. Sucking up the
trickle-down as if you've earned it. It's an outrage.
Isn't it, Col?

COL: [*still below*] Ay?

BAXTER: That's what really makes a bloke glow in
the dark.

COL: [*emerging with a six-pack of beer*] Whassat?

BAXTER: Rage, Col. Rage and indignation.

COL: Ya lost me, son.

BAXTER: Bludgers. Queue jumpers. Bottom feeders.

COL: Too bloody right. Here, heads up.

He lobs a beer across, and then a second.

BAXTER: [*catching the cans, then brandishing them*]
Well caught, that boy! To the humble working
man and his national holiday.

COL: And to those fine men piped ashore already.

BAXTER *sets one beer down and opens the other.*

BAXTER: Come again?

COL: Us, son. No longer on active duty.

He opens his can and swallows greedily.

BAXTER: Oh.

He sips.

COL: Redeployed.

BAXTER: Cashiered, more like. Pensioned off.

COL: I'm no bloody pensioner, comrade, I'm a
self-funded retiree.

BAXTER: That'll explain the cauliflowers.

COL: Five for a dollar at the markets.

BAXTER: Thrifty old salt. What're you gunna do
with five?

COL: Make a curry?

BAXTER: That'll fill your spinnaker.

COL: [*a farting sound*] Prrrt! Man the lifeboats!

BAXTER: As if we haven't got enough wind out here
already. Howls from the east all morning and
blasts you from the south all afternoon.

COL: Died off to nothing now. Hot old night ahead.

BAXTER: Don't you ever feel bullied by it?

COL: The heat?

BAXTER: No, the wind.

COL: Oh, don't be a sook, sailor. Show some pride in ya frontier gale. Might be rough as a pig's tit, but it's ours, and no corn-fed Yank or smartarse Sydney pillow biter can take it off us. And Canberra? Canberra can get stuffed.

BAXTER: Right. That'll be worth fightin for.

COL: Christ, they want everything. Mining royalties, footy players—

BAXTER: But they can't take our hot air, can they Col?

COL: Ours, son! All of it.

BAXTER: Absolutely.

COL: Don't you find yourself invigorated by it?

BAXTER: No, I don't.

COL: Challenged?

BAXTER: In every follicle.

COL: Son, if ya fancy yourself becomin any sort of mariner ya better get to love it. Take ya to the world, that wind. Or bring the world right to ya. [*He inhales ostentatiously.*] Some afternoons

I can smell peri-peri blowin across the water from South Africa.

BAXTER: Sure it's not the rubbish tips of Soweto?

COL: Vanilla beans on Madagascar—

BAXTER: Dream on—

COL: Coconut oil from Mauritius—

BAXTER: The smell of newly minted debt, Col, wafting across the Indian Ocean—

COL: Miserable bastard.

BAXTER: Famine, gun smoke, burning oil. World Bank aftershave.

COL *fishes out a bottle of rum and passes it across by means of a scoop net.*

COL: Happy Australia Day, ya gloomy prick.

BAXTER *looks at the bottle, hesitates, but gulps down several swallows. Both men sit a long moment, each in their own boatload of thoughts.*

BAXTER: You ever been to Africa?

COL: Christ, no. Machete-wieldin maniacs, weevils that swim up your dick. Man'd need a death wish.

He beckons for the bottle back. BAXTER *takes another slug before returning it.*

I'm all for travel, for a fat sail and a full fridge, but a bloke's got his limits.

BAXTER: What about India?

COL: Nup. Partial to a curry, but.

BAXTER: The Maldives? They're on the way.

COL: Ceylon.

BAXTER: Sri Lanka.

COL: That, too.

BAXTER: So many places to go. All out there, Col. When you get that mast back up.

COL: I'll get it up.

BAXTER: Said that last week. And all the weeks before that.

COL: I'll get there. I'll be gone like shit off a shovel.

BAXTER: No doubt.

COL: A few logistical issues, that's all.

BAXTER: Tackled methodically and tirelessly, all the livelong day.

COL: [*bristling*] Remind me, son. What is it that you do all day?

BAXTER: Apart from chasing the lowly blue swimmer crab, welfare cheat of the seabed?

A PASSERBY *in work boots stops on the boardwalk to roll a fag. He takes an interest in* COL's *fallen mast.*

PASSERBY: [*calling*] Brewer's droop.

COL: [*turning to the newcomer*] Ya what?

PASSERBY: Brewer's droop, mate.

BAXTER: Some kind of Masonic password?

PASSERBY: Shoulda called it *Viagra*. Look where goodness gets ya.

COL: Strewth, is that the time?

He manufactures a two-fingered salute from an ostentatious glance at his watch and then turns his back.

PASSERBY: Happy Australia Day.

He lights his fag and leaves.

Wanker.

BAXTER: Must be peaceful out there.

COL: Where?

BAXTER: Out the end.

COL: Moored alongside the plastic gin palaces of the great and the good – and the sorely leveraged?

BAXTER: I spose money buys a bit of distance.

COL: Any other night but tonight, it would.

BAXTER: When did that happen, how did tonight become the highest feast on the liturgical calendar?

COL: Well, there's schoolies week, that's a biggie—

BAXTER: New Year's Eve—

COL: The Rotto Swim—

BAXTER: Anzac Day.

COL: [*slapping his hand over his heart*] Anzac Day.

BAXTER: Do I detect a theme here?

COL: Piss and sunburn?

BAXTER: More like youth and folly.

COL: [*surveying the junk suspended from* BAXTER'*s rigging*] Speakin of folly . . . I see you've been dragging the harbour again. The bike's a find.

BAXTER: 1968 or thereabouts. The banana seat's seen better days.

COL: Where the hell do they come from?

BAXTER: The sea gives up her dead, eventually.

COL: And sends them to you. You're a shit-magnet.

BAXTER: So I'm told.

COL: What, you gunna fix 'em and sell 'em?

BAXTER: Nah, they just . . . I dunno, remind me of stuff.

COL: And that's the sum total of the day's activity? Collecting crap and reminiscing on other crap?

BAXTER: I did try to string up a hammock.

COL: Like tits on a bull, you are.

BAXTER: If bulls had tits they'd be nervous in your paddock, Col.

COL: Ha!

BAXTER: I'm right here, day and night. You know what I do. It's pretty much what you do, and that's five-eighths of bugger-all.

COL: Speak for yourself.

BAXTER: Alright then—

COL: I'm layin in provisions, preparing to make a passage.

BAXTER: Well, ahoy and avast and good on ya. But me, I'm under no illusions. [*Agitated now, he drains off his beer and crushes the can.*] I'm staying right here where it's calm.

Along the boardwalk, a REVELLER, *drinking rum from a half-empty bottle and toting an esky daubed in the flag's colours, takes an interest in the older men.*

Safe and predictable's all I'm after.

REVELLER: Christ, look at that filthy tub. Give it a scrape, Grandad!

BAXTER: [*surprised and offended*] I think he means me.

COL: Fuck off! Cashed-up bogans, that's all we need.

REVELLER: Old turd.

The REVELLER *moves off.*

BAXTER: And may your . . . mother go to the Himalayas!

COL: [*laughing derisively*] Christ, Baxter, that's feeble.

BAXTER: Well said, that boy!

He raises his beer in salute but his mood is slipping.

REVELLER: [*off*] Aussie, Aussie, Aussie!

BOATIES: [*off*] Oi, oi, oi!

The sounds of revelry rise and fall. Car horns, a stereo booms a phrase of Men at Work's 'Down Under'.

BAXTER: They're at it early tonight.

COL: Half the town's pissed already.

BAXTER: The rest are just pissed off.

COL: And in four hours we'll all be both.

BAXTER: Partying hard, I believe it's called.

COL: Ah, I don't mind a bit of a fiesta.

BAXTER: Fiasco.

COL: Look at ya. Like a bloke who's just sucked the guts out of a lemon. Bracin yourself to start in on a grapefruit.

BAXTER *laughs. He gets up and pulls in another crab-line. Nothing. He lowers it back.*

What're you usin for bait?

BAXTER: Spleen.

COL: Spleen.

BAXTER: Spleen.

COL: Poor buggers. On top of every other environmental and evolutionary indignity you serve 'em up spleen.

BAXTER: Bottom feeders, Col. Thought you'd approve.

COL: You got no sense of humour.

BAXTER: Spleen. Yes, I see what I'm missing. What time's the fireworks?

COL: Nine. Eight. Something like that.

BAXTER: What is it about fire crackers and national spirit?

COL: Everyone fancies a good bang and a bit of a smoke afterwards.

BAXTER: Yes, that's what made this country great.

COL: Don't see you flyin the flag there.

BAXTER: Well, where's yours?

COL: Look at me mast, son. You've got no excuse.

BAXTER: Oh, don't start.

COL: I'm not startin anythin.

BAXTER: Never a truer word spoken.

COL: Impudent, you are, son. Drinkin a man's beer.

BAXTER: Said you'd be gone by Christmas.

COL: Well, you saw what happened.

BAXTER: I did.

COL: Well. Things happen at sea.

BAXTER: It didn't exactly come down in a gale on the high seas, Col; you dropped it. You were tied up to the jetty at the time, full of Bundy and EB.

COL: Orright, it got away from me . . . have to rub it in.

BAXTER: Nearly killed Bedford Grainger.

COL: That white-shoe prick, I'd have been a hero on this jetty.

BAXTER: Never seen a man with gout run so fast.

COL: Draggin an esky and a mistress, no less.

BAXTER: Imagine the obituaries. What a murky melange of arse-licking and moral outrage they'd be.

COL: If I'da killed him?

BAXTER: WA Ink Dry at Last.

COL: Fat, swindling prick.

BAXTER: Rent in two by a mere drunken fumble.

COL: All the dirty secrets in 'im. Be like a bomb goin off.

BAXTER: Boom!

COL: Shit and indiscretion everywhere.

BAXTER: Wasn't even that close, really.

COL: More's the pity. Worth seein the fear in his face, but.

BAXTER: Anyway, you'll be gone come Anzac Day.

COL: Yeah.

BAXTER: Life on the ocean wave.

COL: Yep. Unencumbered. No whinin kids, no
needy wife, no mortgage. Free as a franger.

They finish their beers. COL *goes below for more beer.* BAXTER
surveys COL's *broken boat.*

BAXTER: Good old Col.

COL: [*off*] Ow. Shit!

BAXTER: Cooks up voyages of an evening and
farts 'em out like cauliflower curry before dawn.
Every rope rotted onto its cleat. But the dream
never fades.

*Beneath him, on the water, gradually illuminated in his little
dinghy, the* BOY *watches and listens. Sounds of muted laughter,
champagne corks, sizzling barbecues.*

Always leaving, never gone. Every cell in you says
go, change, run away, but you can't muster the
steam and steel to actually shoot through. Smell
that? Fried hopes, grilled expectations. Oops, not
too burnt, is it, not a fussy bugger, are ya, don't
mind, do ya? Nah, nah, nah, I'm right, I'm fine,
no flies on me – the usual bluster and bullshit.
While the marriage fails, the company tanks, the
career and reputation go down the shitter. Look

at us here, the faded beauties and jaded smarties.
Kids won't talk, the brokers don't call, and now
it's malignant this and squamous that . . . so why
wouldn't you hole up and hide out? The easily
replaced and internally displaced – why wouldn't
we want to piss off and start again, answer to
another name entirely?

The BOY *closes in on* BAXTER, *steadies himself against
the bigger boat and stands barely an arm's length away. As*
BAXTER *talks he moves along the gunwale, comes aboard
behind him and inspects the deck as if it's his own future or
perhaps his past.*

Of course down here we're uniquely placed to
capitalise on synergies going forward. When
the last slab of ice shelf flops over and the acid
ocean surges our way, we'll be as ready as anyone.
Every one of us'll be Noah, loading our regrets,
two-by-two, arked-up for oblivion. And our
strategy in the face of cataclysm? Buy more rope,
shipmates! What do we do? Nada.

He tries to tie a bowline.

See, Col, that's what I do all day; I hunker down
in Happy Land like the rest of them. Ahoy and
how's it goin. Safe, quiet, immobile. Now, how
does this go again? The rabbit comes out of the
hole and round the log and . . . [*Throwing it*

aside] As luck would have it, here's something
I prepared earlier.

*From a basket he takes a hangman's noose. He pulls it over his
head. Horrified, the* BOY *tries to restrain him but he's powerless.
Relenting,* BAXTER *rotates the loop until he's wearing the knot
like a tie. He moves forward as though to a mirror and adjusts it
while the* BOY *laughs in relief, fades, and is gone.*

Believe me, though, I think about it. But like Col,
I make plans and carefully fail to execute them.

*Offstage, the slam of a car door. A thud of something heavy
hitting the ground. The squeal of tyres and bawl of an engine as
the car races away. A woman bellows out of sight in a cockney
accent.* DEE, *a nineteen-year-old backpacker, enters, very drunk.*

DEE: That's it, drive away! You weak little tosser!
Fuckin tosser! Fuckin toerag! Pillock! You filthy,
weak bastard!

COL: Look out, ducks on the pond.

DEE *totters along the boardwalk with her rucksack. More than
once she almost goes into the water and the spectacle of her
strange, perilous dance distracts* BAXTER *from his maudlin
train of thought.*

DEE: You! Are! A! Total! Cunt! [*Tearful*] Cunts like
you give cunts a bad name.

COL *comes up on deck in a fresh, loud shirt, looking bathed, bearing more drinks. He passes the bottle of rum to* BAXTER *who accepts, distracted, while dropping his noose into the basket on deck and watching the inebriated newcomer. Takes a swig and passes it back.*

COL: The fuckin language!

BAXTER: Cheers.

He opens the can he's been saving.

COL: Can't help but notice, neighbour, but in the last few weeks you've drunk a lot of my beer.

BAXTER: Well, you keep offering. And your beer's cold.

COL: So why is it that your beer never seems to migrate to the cooler climes of my functioning fridge? Don't even buy ice, ya lazy prick. Don't cook, don't work on ya boat—

BAXTER: [*as a diversion, a toast*] To the baggy green!

COL: [*automatically, despite himself*] The baggy green.

BAXTER: Warnie!

COL: Warnie!

BAXTER: Juddy!

COL: Pav!

BAXTER: To whatsisname, the bloke down the road
    there who won the Nobel Prize for—

COL: Bugger him. Anyway, ya changing the subject.
    I'm talkin beverages.

DEE *teeters, pulls off her rucksack and sits heavily on it.
Muttering silently, she sways at the boardwalk's edge. Together
the men watch her progress.*

BAXTER: Speaking of beverages . . . she's gunna go
    over in a minute.

COL: One less tourist.

BAXTER: Come on, Col, you'd be down to the
    Y-fronts in a nanosecond, all chest and chin, like
    a North-Cott clubby doing the righty.

COL: Hn. Maybe. If she was good-lookin. [*Peering*]
    She good-lookin?

DEE *staggers up to go through her pockets and as she does she
almost goes in.*

Oopsy-daisy.

BAXTER: [*to* DEE] Hey, you orright there?

DEE: Piss off.

COL: Think you're in with a chance there, son.

DEE: [*in tears*] Fuck!

COL: Classy.

BAXTER: She's in no fit state.

COL: Don't get involved.

DEE *struggles to her feet and falls flat, almost going over the side. To* COL's *great amusement,* BAXTER *leaps up onto the jetty, pushes back the gate and scuttles over to where* DEE *is trying to haul herself up in a sobbing, drunken rage.*

BAXTER: Here, steady on, love. You'll end up in the drink. So to speak.

DEE: Lemme alone. Call the fuckin cops.

BAXTER: Hey, you're bleeding. You've taken some bark off, there.

DEE: Get your soddin hands off me.

BAXTER: Listen, have you got something to—?

DEE: I'm fine, yeah? So, fuck off, lemme go.

BAXTER: Why don't I walk you back up to the street there, away from the water? I'll give you a hand with your pack.

COL: Come back here, ya drongo, she's probably on drugs!

BAXTER: Oh, dry up, Col.

COL: Suit yourself, ya dopy shit-magnet.

DEE *and* BAXTER *continue tussling mutely up and down the boardwalk. Light on* COL.

Never know if I wanna drown him or give him
    the shirt off me back. No idea how to get on in
    the world, not a practical bone in his body, but
    a good-hearted boy. Ya want to steer him right.
    But Christ he's an earnest bugger, way he talks
    himself into a mood. Pop your head on deck and
    there he is like a rain-bearin depression, workin
    his way toward some kinda bloody deluge a man
    can't even guess at. He bought the old *Shirley*
    there sight unseen – definitely her best angle.
    What a dog. And there he was – two milk crates
    of books and an air of wounded virtue. Just

showed up last winter, like a ghost of himself, the
way they do, boltin from the law, the wife, the
tax man, something. They think it'll be all cosy
and private down here, but they've never lived
a fathom away from all their neighbours before,
where you can't even take a leak without half
the jetty knowin. Live like this, it's gotta be: see
no evil, hear no evil, and . . . well, speak as little
evil as you can manage. Take Jackie over there;
that girlie on the old sloop. She knows her port
from her starboard. Must have a few bob, 'cause
that boat's a work of art; rebuilt like a Claremont
soccer mum. I get all goosey just looking at it.
She plays her cards close to her chest Jackie, and
fair enough. Decent girl, but beneath the silk
blouse she's all jarrah planks.

Lights up on BAXTER *and* DEE *on the boardwalk. He dangles
his feet over the side and she sits unsteadily on her pack, holding
a bandana to her brow.*

BAXTER: So, there's no one you can call?

DEE: Only him and his cow of a sister. Can't believe
he just . . . left me here. Got no cash left, dunno
where I even am. Australia Day – Christ. Makes
me laugh.

BAXTER: Where's his sister's place?

DEE: Oh, I dunno. Like, fifty miles up the freeway.
Some horrible, sandy, treeless nothing with
the price tags still flappin. Tuscan villas, yeah?
Gangsta pads. Frank Lloyd Wrong.

BAXTER: Don't knock the humble starter castle.
That's someone's dream, love.

DEE: A bloody movie set, I shit you not. Astroturf,
palm trees and wall-to-wall Brits.

BAXTER: Tourists, eh.

DEE: *The Truman Show* starring Ray Winstone and
Posh Spice.

BAXTER: Oh, come on.

DEE: Nah, nah, it was fuckin horrible.

BAXTER: Such a snob.

DEE: Homeless, I am. Can't afford to be a snob.

BAXTER: Well, there's plenty of backpacker joints
across the road there. Follow the trail of bedbugs
and prophylactics.

DEE: You deaf or summink? I'm skint.

Along the boardwalk a bare-chested youth with his shirt tied around his head and a flag draped around him like a cape throws a bottle that smashes in the distance.

BOOFHEAD: Aussie, Aussie, Aussie!

REVELLER: Oi, oi, oi!

He reaches BAXTER *and* DEE.

BOOFHEAD: Bit old for ya, babe, isn't he?

DEE: Fuck off. And don't call me babe, you ugly convict bastard.

BAXTER: Listen, mate—

BOOFHEAD: [*toeing the rucksack*] Got the saddle, where's ya horse?

DEE: I said piss off.

BOOFHEAD: Silly bitch. Just a joke.

DEE: What a talent.

BOOFHEAD: Listen, love, I grew here, you flew here. Go home, ya pommy moll.

DEE: That's the plan, you mouth-breathin moron.

The BOOFHEAD *winds up to kick* DEE*'s pack but misses altogether and tries to disguise it by swinging on his heel and reeling away.* BAXTER *gets to his feet but the lout has already stumbled off and he's spared the manly duty. A diesel starts nearby. Laughter. A stereo cranks up. A ship's horn sounds. More diesels. The entire marina is stirring.*

COL: The circus begins! Every prick and his flush
uncle's gotta have a boat. Whatever happened to the
humble caravan, the modest week at the Bali Four
Seasons, the unassuming three-storey weekender
at Eagle Bay? Got it, had it, lost it in the divorce.
But now they must have The Vessel. Once it was
just the Titans of the Terrace with the fifty-foot
Bertram and the mooring at Rotto. Now it's every
aspirational roo dog with a sniff of blood and a bit
of front, and none of 'em, rich or poor, has the first
fuckin clue what they're doin on the water.

Sounds of anthems and jingo-jingles.

And tonight? Tonight they're up the river for the
fireworks. Simple folk, love our crackers. City
backdrop. FM soundtrack. Liquored-in, rafted-
up, lacquered-over, anchored across each other
like chain-knittin halfwits, whoopin it up like
savages. And the moment the last hunger's fallen
to the teeming, bottle-gougin foreshore, they're
chargin back downriver in the dark in charge of
ten tons of diesel and plastic. Char-issst!

Horns blast. Engines roar. Collisions. COL *snatches up a lifejacket and worms into it.*

> SKIPPER: [*off*] Oops! Sorry, mate.

> COL: Ya bloody knucklehead. Go astern!

> SKIPPER: [*off*] Is that, like, starboard?

> COL: Fuckin wood duck.

> SKIPPER: [*off*] Coming through!

Grinding contact. Wildly reversing diesels. An almighty splintering crash. Splashes and screams, maniacal laughter.

> COL: The west at play. [*Disgusted*] Fuckin fantastic!

Light on BAXTER *and* DEE.

> BAXTER: Maybe you better come and sit on the boat while you're trying to sort yourself out. Might be a bit safer.

> DEE: [*scornfully*] Yeah, right.

> BAXTER: Suit yourself.

> DEE: I fuckin will, too, Grandpa. Just lemme alone.

BAXTER *retreats to his boat. The sounds of revelry, departing boats, horns.* DEE *finds a half-drunk can of beer on the jetty beside her. She shakes it, drains it off, belches and begins to sing drunkenly, gradually giving in to tears.*

> That's when good neighbours . . . become . . .
>   good . . . fuck this place.

She hurls the can and it clatters against JACKIE's *boat, and a light goes on in the cabin.*

Lights down. A hissing barbecue.

Lights up on the Goodness *where* COL *is cooking snags on a barbecue bolted to his transom rail.* BAXTER *emerges, sniffing.*

COL: Christ, I'm hungry.

BAXTER: Yeah, I'm peckish.

COL: I could eat the crutch out of a low-flyin duck.

BAXTER: Indeed.

COL: I could eat Phar Lap, glass case and all.

BAXTER: Hoofs and hide.

COL: Teeth and tongue.

BAXTER: Tail and testicles.

COL: I'm so hungry . . . I'm so hungry I could eat
a boiled baby.

*Both men are brought up short by this infelicitous image.
COL is chastened by the silence.*

I'm famished, that's all I'm sayin.

DEE *totters up the jetty in the sombre moment.*

Oh, look out. Seagulls!

DEE *pauses at* BAXTER's *boat and heaves her pack onto
his deck.*

DEE: Permission to—

DEE *falls aboard, rolls over, and begins to snore.*

BAXTER: Um . . .

COL: Bloody hell.

BAXTER: Yes.

COL: Look at that. Tatts and studs all over her.
Yeah-nah, close-up she's a looker. If you don't

mind 'em slightly shopsoiled and smellin of Bacardi and BO.

JACKIE *emerges on deck.*

Look out! Hide yer manly secrets. It's the mistress of *Mercy.*

JACKIE: God, an endless day just got longer.

COL: Don't be like that.

JACKIE: Talk about a cure for homesickness. Heckle and Jeckle.

COL: What time'd you get in?

JACKIE: What are you, my father?

BAXTER: You eaten? You look a bit peaky.

JACKIE: Let me get this right. Which one of you's the dad and who's the mother?

COL: Comrades, to the bunker!

BAXTER: How was Shanghai?

JACKIE: Shenzhen.

BAXTER: How was it?

JACKIE: Almost as depressing as the sight of you two.

COL: Ha! Jetlag, the Curse – there's always somethin.

BAXTER: I'm not that depressing.

JACKIE: Tell him, Col.

COL: Well, son, you do—

JACKIE: Girl gets home from a week of vicious philanthropy to discover once more that charity begins at home.

COL: But you can't find charity enough in yer heart to make room for ole Col. Can ya?

JACKIE: Sex god that you are, Col, I find my diary suddenly filled up. And bile lapping green at the back of my throat.

BAXTER: I can't be that depressing.

JACKIE: Stop dwelling on it, Baxter, you'll only make it worse for all of us. God, it's hot.

BAXTER: [*reaching for a can*] Col's got beer.

COL: Yeah, that'd be right. Col's got beer.

JACKIE: Nah, I'm right, but I could go a snag, while you're buying.

COL: What'm I, camp uncle?

JACKIE: Col, you're old enough to be whatever you have to be; I'm broadminded.

She takes her jacket from the boom, goes into her cabin and calls back.

Don't stay in the closet on my account! God knows, no woman'd have you.

COL: You should change the name of that boat, girlie. No mercy from that quarter.

BAXTER: What's this foundation she works for?

COL: I dunno, some do-goodin thing. Flies business class.

BAXTER: She meditates, you know.

COL: [*appalled*] Christ.

BAXTER: Out on deck of a morning.

COL: Well, she's a stand-up sheila in my book, even
     if she does play for the other team.

BAXTER: That a fact?

COL: Tough, tarred and watertight. And, Christ,
     a tongue that'd strip the freckles off a ranga.

JACKIE *comes back on deck with a glass of juice and a plate
of snacks. She surveys her neighbours who are suddenly
dumbstruck.*

     Juice!

JACKIE: Squeezed it myself.

The plate of snags travels from boat to boat.

BAXTER: Using organic fair trade produce, I hope.

JACKIE: The oranges are local.

BAXTER: Oh, well. No one's perfect.

COL *and* BAXTER *watch the shadow of a bird on the water.*

COL: That's a night heron.

BAXTER: Really?

COL: Beautiful, beautiful bird.

Along the jetty comes RAY, *a fellow jetty rat, wheeling a barrow full of food and jingling bottles. He wears a hat and shirt emblazoned with the Australian flag.* RAY *pulls up near* COL's *boat and sets the laden barrow down. He pulls out a long, flowing flag on a stick and waves it in elaborate arcs.*

RAY: Ahoy, ladies.

COL: G'day, Ray.

RAY: Aussie, Aussie, Aussie!

COL: Oi, oi, oi!

JACKIE: Oh, please.

RAY: Seems to be an obstruction on the jetty. Still.

COL: Yeah, alright, I'm comin. Man's gotta be
    caterin service, sage and mule.

COL *clambers up onto the jetty, a snag in one hand, and helps* RAY *heave the barrow across the obstruction of the mast.* JACKIE *and* BAXTER *fade into the evening gloom.*

RAY: Geez, Col, it's not exactly a groundbreakin feat of engineerin getting this bloody thing back up, you know.

COL: Yeah, but I got a lotta things on, son. Besides, I think it's got a kink in it.

RAY: Oh, bullshit. Three blokes, a block and tackle, new plate and pin. [*Conspiratorially*] Did I see a girl?

COL: It's his niece.

RAY: Pull the other one.

COL: Nah, he's orright.

RAY: Not what I heard.

COL: What about hear no evil?

RAY: Man's got ears, nothing you can do about it.

COL: Everyone on this jetty's made a meal of things sometime or other. It's WA, mate, what about a fair go and a third chance?

RAY: Yeah, but . . . He ever taken that bloody thing outta the pen?

COL: He knows the pointy end's the front, but
Joshua Slocum he is not.

RAY: Christ, it's a disgrace.

COL: Took her out the once. Gets beyond the
breakwater, slap into the southerly, frightens the
tripe out of himself. Boat sails itself backwards
into the harbour, flappin like a cockatiel. Nah,
mate, all he wants is a caravan that floats. No
harm in that.

RAY: Wants more'n that, mate. He wants
horsewhippin.

COL: What're you talking about? Ahead of his time,
that's all.

Light on BAXTER *and* JACKIE *in mute conversation,
oblivious.*

RAY: Ahead of you, I reckon. Carn, me beer's getting
warm.

COL *helps* RAY *lift the wheelbarrow across the fallen mast.*

COL: Is that tequila? O fuckin lay!

*As they exit stage left the light is almost gone from the sky and
stars have begun to show.*

JACKIE: Look at our flag, a Union Jack with a five-star review!

BAXTER: Once upon a time, except for the inside of a courthouse, you'd hardly see a flag in this country.

JACKIE: Have you noticed the flagpoles turning up in people's front yards? They fly the flag every day of the year. Like Americans.

BAXTER: Yes, I've seen it.

JACKIE: Gives me the creeps.

BAXTER: Spose there's no harm in a bit of national pride.

JACKIE: There's something forced about it, aggressive. Like: 'I'm more patriotic than you and if you were any sort of Australian you'd fly it, too. Higher, harder.'

BAXTER: Sounds a little paranoid, don't you think?

JACKIE: People used to pride themselves on being indifferent to that sort of thing. We used to be suspicious of claptrap.

BAXTER: Well, at the risk of sounding like the schoolteacher I was, we did, in 1915, with extreme enthusiasm, send a generation of farm boys to Gallipoli and the Somme. Boys in their thousands. We've fertilised plenty of foreign soil with blood and bones, Jackie. Mostly in the name of pure claptrap. So, I can't say I detect any historical immunity to flag-waving bullshit.

JACKIE: Could you possibly sound more pompous?

BAXTER: Well, there, young lass, I imagine I could, yes.

JACKIE: It's not that you don't feel pride, now and then, at the sight of the national flag.

BAXTER: When, exactly? Aside from the Olympics.

JACKIE: Oh, I dunno. Timor? Aceh after the tsunami.

BAXTER: But.

JACKIE: Yeah, but. I find it uncomfortable.

BAXTER: I don't know what you mean.

JACKIE: Really? You don't feel anxious when you see it brandished all day every day?

BAXTER: But it's the national day.

JACKIE: You don't ever feel a bit ambivalent?

BAXTER: How could you feel ambivalent about
your own flag?

JACKIE: Well, how does the flag make you feel,
Baxter?

BAXTER: Proud.

JACKIE: Proud?

BAXTER: And excited. I want to drink vast amounts
of piss and get sunstroke and run screaming
through the streets with the flag pouring off my
shoulders like a superhero's rippling cape while
I go after wogs and slopes and towel-head reffos
and bash their fuckin heads in.

After a long traumatic beat, JACKIE *begins to laugh.*

JACKIE: You rotten bugger, you had me going.

BAXTER: I did.

JACKIE: I thought – Jesus, I don't know this man
at all.

BAXTER: And you were correct.

JACKIE: No, I was . . . discombobulated.

BAXTER: Yeah, get used to that feeling.

JACKIE: Discombobulation. What a lovely word for something so unlovely.

BAXTER: Take this girl, this young voyager, for instance.

JACKIE: [*alarmed*] What girl?

BAXTER: This one. She's got a tattoo in the small of her back. Got me well and truly discombobulated.

JACKIE: Who's she?

BAXTER: No idea.

JACKIE: What, she just grew there? Like a barnacle?

BAXTER: Found her wandering up the boardwalk.

JACKIE: A street kid?

BAXTER: Backpacker, had a blue with the fella, reckons she's broke, nowhere to go. She's got

a tattoo in the small of her back, it's got me in
a spin.

JACKIE: Every little girl's got one there, now, Baxter.
It's where it is that's got you in a spin.

BAXTER: In Gothic script, this tattoo. 'Pogrom', it
says.

JACKIE: What?

BAXTER: Pogrom. P-O-G-R-O-M. Pogrom.

JACKIE: Jesus.

BAXTER: You think she even knows what it means?

JACKIE: Why is she even here? What were you
thinking of, having her aboard?

BAXTER: She sort of invited herself, and to tell you
the truth, I was going to ask whether you'd take
her in for the night.

JACKIE: Me?

BAXTER: Well, it's awkward.

JACKIE: You're bloody right it's awkward.

BAXTER: For me, I mean.

JACKIE: And not for me?

BAXTER: You don't understand.

JACKIE: I understand perfectly. Shit, Baxter.

BAXTER: You see, the whole jetty will—

JACKIE: And you think they won't be talking if she stays with me?

BAXTER: [*bewildered*] Well.

JACKIE: I've got something on tonight. How old is she?

BAXTER: Couldn't say.

JACKIE: I'm sure you could make an educated guess.

BAXTER: Well . . . she can't be much more than twenty.

JACKIE: What's she like?

BAXTER: Come and see for yourself.

JACKIE: See? Tell me, Baxter. What's she like?

BAXTER: Oh. Well. Long, dark hair. Good skin, for her age. Pretty face, despite the hunk of metal in her chin. Um . . . [*indicating breasts haplessly*] . . . stud in the bellybutton. How'm I doing?

JACKIE: I dunno. How d'you think you're doing?

BAXTER: Bit hard to say.

JACKIE: Really?

BAXTER: She could do with a shower. Authentic backpacker pong, that's for sure.

JACKIE: You haven't described her legs, Baxter. Or what about her arse?

DEE *stirs a moment before lapsing back into a stupor.*

DEE: Fuggin tosser.

BAXTER: Where's Col gotten to?

JACKIE: You were a teacher?

BAXTER: Who told you I was a teacher?

JACKIE: You did. A few moments ago.

BAXTER: Oh. That was . . . indiscreet.

JACKIE: What did you teach?

BAXTER: What's gotten into you?

JACKIE: Today. Tonight. [*Gesturing towards* DEE] This. Anyway, it didn't strike me as a particularly intrusive question.

BAXTER *hesitates, fidgets, twangs his safety lines.*

BAXTER: Geography.

JACKIE: Geography . . . Baxter, we have all these conversations—

BAXTER: When you're in the mood for them.

JACKIE: We have all these neighbourly conversations—

BAXTER: Well, it's the neighbourly national day of self-congratulation, when we thank God we're not in Zimbabwe or Burma or Afghanistan—

JACKIE: And, really, honestly—

BAXTER: Or . . . living in a country where infants have chlamydia and scabies and live in squalor so unthinkable as to—

JACKIE: Jesus, Baxter—

BAXTER: But enough of that. A few crackers, a bit of Anzackery, and a reading from the Apostle Bradman – brings out the neighbour in a bloke.

JACKIE: We keep having all these conversations and yet you never tell me anything important about yourself.

BAXTER: See, I not only feel disappointment, I propagate it. It metastasises all around me.

JACKIE: Your wife, tell me—

BAXTER: What makes you think I was ever married?

JACKIE: Must be the haunted look.

BAXTER: Ah, that.

JACKIE: Where is she?

BAXTER: Who?

JACKIE: Mrs Baxter.

BAXTER: She's dead, Jackie.

JACKIE: Oh. I'm sorry.

BAXTER: You really are a lot of fun tonight, you know that?

JACKIE: Sorry to disappoint.

BAXTER: Me too. Jackie, our home is girt by sea.

JACKIE: And what the hell does that mean?

BAXTER: You know the jetty protocol.

JACKIE: Crap on and say nothing.

BAXTER: Why not? It works. Even for you, especially you. One way or another we've, all of us, slunk down here to lick our wounds.

JACKIE: You blokes'd lick your own balls if you had the flexibility.

BAXTER: Guilty as charged, but the fact is that we can't, and having found ourselves lonely, we just want to be left alone. What part of that is confusing to you?

JACKIE: I'm not confused, I'm dissatisfied.

BAXTER: Now you're a philosopher.

JACKIE: And you're being a turd.

BAXTER: Very likely. But I learnt jetty manners from you, neighbour. I watched and imitated. And hey, it works, and it seemed to suit you fine. Until tonight. Even on the water, fences'll make good neighbours, Jack. No need to set off a torrent of confession. God knows where that'd lead.

JACKIE: And what about intimacy?

BAXTER: Jackie! Don't forget, I watch you too. Flying out, slipping back. Talking into the Huckleberry—

JACKIE: BlackBerry, you goose—

BAXTER: Maybe it's drugs, I tell myself—

JACKIE: Don't be ridiculous—

BAXTER: Or just keeping the world at bay. None of my business.

JACKIE: Damn right.

BAXTER: You don't want intimacy. Your heart is girt by a sea – of pack ice.

JACKIE: Well, thank you!

BAXTER: You've figured out what's no longer safe and
you've carried what's left of yourself down here
and you'll guard it with your life – I respect that.

JACKIE: Aw, an elephant stamp from the teacher.

BAXTER: But you don't want intimacy. You just
fancy a little bit of information. Just as I was
lulled into my false sense of obscurity, along
comes Jackie of the good ship *Mercy*, always
knowing more than she lets on.

JACKIE: Christ, you've got a nerve!

BAXTER: No, you're one of life's gleaners. You know
who's on parole, who's in remission. I kind of
admire it. A bloke wouldn't apply himself with so
much discipline.

JACKIE: Fuck you!

BAXTER: Well, you wanted something more,
comrade, something real. To quote an uplifting
bumper sticker I saw yesterday: 'HARDEN THE
FUCK UP'.

JACKIE: I'm pack ice already, remember?

BAXTER: Sorry. It's the beer talking. And the Bundy
might have been a mistake.

JACKIE: Baxter, it's never the booze talking. It's the drunk. It's the dickhead within.

BAXTER: Maybe you're right.

JACKIE: Believe me, I'm right.

BAXTER: Do I detect an air of authority, a weary note of experience?

JACKIE *begins to fidget, refuses to engage.*

And that now you've brought it up—

JACKIE: I didn't bring it up—

BAXTER: You've never raised a loaded glass on this jetty in all the months I've been here. And I've never once had the audacity to ask you – are you or are you not a recovering alcoholic, or are you dieting for the sake of your girlfriend in Brussels?

JACKIE *retreats to her cabin to leave* BAXTER *alone beneath the starlit sky.*

Oh, well said, that boy! You bloody idiot.

DEE: [*asleep*] Fuckin brussels sprouts . . .

BAXTER *looks at* DEE, *ponders.*

BAXTER: On your sacred bachelor deck you find
a girl.

DEE *rises behind him.*

DEE: It smells of tar and beer and rotting meat,
like old people. And the world's just rocking,
voices swirling, like they're all still talking across
you. With their tone of authority, makes 'em
sound like they're in control, they'll always be in
control. Even if they're fakin it.

JACKIE *emerges on deck, hesitating with the tray of food she
has prepared.*

BAXTER: Welcome, my dear, with your backpack
full of shoes and rancid laundry, your half-read
copy of *Shantaram* and your juice-bottle bong.
Your sweaty London scalp. The *'arbeit macht
frei'* on your gorgeous, gorgeous little arse. Just
lie back and take up space, blossom; you're safe
from me.

JACKIE: Stewart Baxter. Pudding Club High. For
a moment there he was a kind of celebrity,
a bloke doing his best to keep pregnant girls
in school out there in Struggle Town. Set up
a creche in the demountable art room. Fought off
the bureaucrats, bent the rules, caught people's
imagination. If he'd been fifteen years younger,

with a ponytail and an earring, nobody would have given him a moment's thought. He'd be just another trendy wanker. But here's Mr Baxter in his grey strides with his specs on a string and his shirt buttoned up crooked. A ratepayer. Every social trend since sweet and sour pork has passed him by unnoticed. And all he wants is a fair go for struggling girls. The media couldn't get enough of him.

BAXTER *is startled to see realise that* JACKIE *has been listening. He gestures toward the foredeck.*

BAXTER: Ah. Children, eh? Angels when they're asleep.

Sceptical, JACKIE *proffers a plate and he nods and takes it from her across the short divide between boats.*

Hmm, they look good. Vietnamese?

JACKIE: For God's sake, just eat.

BAXTER: I'm sorry. About before. I apologise. Really. Why don't you come aboard?

JACKIE: It's crowded there already.

BAXTER: This plate is staying here, so if you want any you'd better come aboard.

Still clutching her glass, JACKIE *hops across from her boat to his. She settles herself against a rail and raises her glass to him ironically.*

Cheers.

JACKIE: Yeah.

BAXTER: I've got two kids, you know.
Twenty-eight and thirty. She's in Hong Kong
and he's in Sydney somewhere, I gather.

JACKIE: You don't have to—

BAXTER: Estranged. Such a pastel word, eh? Doesn't
quite cover the savagery and the recrimination.
We had an untidy divorce and then there were
mortal complications.

JACKIE: Kids find it hard to forgive, after a certain
age. A father leaving them.

BAXTER: I was asked to leave. Turfed out, actually.

JACKIE: We needn't talk about it.

BAXTER: Needn't we?

JACKIE: You're drunk.

BAXTER: Exactly. See, it was her having the affair – and suddenly I'm out on the street.

JACKIE: Listen, Baxter, really—

BAXTER: Next day the interloper moves in. And get this, I later discover that my daughter holds it against me that I didn't fight hard enough to stay. Lost respect, she says. [*With a laugh*] Jesus!

JACKIE: Well, kids are complicated.

BAXTER: And their parents are, what, simple?

JACKIE: I take it there's been no late-life reconciliation?

BAXTER: No, it got worse. I let the wife keep the house, of course, but when she died – breast cancer, the poor beggar – she gave it back to me.

JACKIE: You make it sound like it was yours to give.

BAXTER: Alright, she bequeathed the full share to me. Me. Happy?

JACKIE: Why not to the kids?

BAXTER: I dunno, maybe because they hadn't worked for thirty years to pay off the mortgage.

JACKIE: So you expected it.

BAXTER: Of course I didn't – Christ. But . . .
the kids thought I'd robbed them of their
inheritance – a chocolate-brick bungalow in
shady Gosnells, for pity's sake.

JACKIE: You kicked them out?

BAXTER: Of course not. They wouldn't stay under
the same roof with me. I was persona non grata
by then, and not just with them.

JACKIE: Oh?

BAXTER: Bit of a kerfuffle at the funeral.

JACKIE: A kerfuffle.

BAXTER: I was under a lot of stress.

JACKIE: At work.

BAXTER: How'm I doing here? Is this raw and
personal enough?

JACKIE: Eat something.

BAXTER: Even when her treachery was fresh, those
nights when I lay weeping in the dry bathtub of

my fleabag renter, cursing the ground she walked
on, I still loved her—

JACKIE: In my way—

BAXTER: Well, it's true! And all the years
that followed, in my long, grey, impotent
bachelorhood – it never wore off. So I took
her death . . . untidily. And by then, of course,
the wheels were well and truly off my little red
wagon. Hey, let me tell you about the funeral—

JACKIE: Eat!

BAXTER: No, no, listen, you won't believe this.

JACKIE: I don't need to believe anything—

BAXTER: So, we're all at the graveside, right, just
after the committal when everyone's tipping
in their dollop of dirt, and I'm overtaken by
a peculiar impulse – now think of this tonight,
Jackie, while you're bunked down six feet away
from a madman; can't believe I'm telling you
this—

JACKIE: Here, eat.

BAXTER: Now, you're rattled!

JACKIE: Correct.

BAXTER: Hm, they do look good, these. Where was I? Ah, right. I approach the open grave, and all eyes are on me, the limp pariah. I take off the stylish Cancer Council sunglasses and let them fall. Into the grave, the homely acid dirt of the Swan coastal plain. From the pockets, two parking tickets, a dry-cleaning stub, a spearmint Lifesaver. Murmur murmur. I slip off the jacket and bombs away, unbutton the shirt and down it flutters. Gasp and grumble grumble. Kick off the Windsor Smiths – left and right – and in they go. Socks away! Dropped the strides – I kid you not – car keys, wallet and all, and hoiked 'em in.

JACKIE: Baxter.

BAXTER: And by the time it comes down to the mighty whities, which were no laundering triumph at the time, I'm howling my eyes out. I'm gone for all money. So why would I leave it at that? Of course, I go all the way. And I probably would've jumped into the hole right there and then, down into the hot, grey Bassendean sands, if it hadn't simply looked like I was having second thoughts about the Visa card and the keys to the Falcon. I was, quite literally, beside myself – I could see myself doing all this mad shit – flaming with sorrow, self-pity, pain.

Funeral director fella's kindly slipped his coat
over my shoulders and led me away like I'm
a streaker at the cricket.

The celebratory hubbub rises around them.

That little scene came back to haunt me, I can tell
you. 'Evidence of my instability.' But the feeling
was real. The pain was real.

JACKIE: What was her name?

BAXTER: No.

JACKIE: The wife.

BAXTER: I can't say it.

JACKIE: That scheme you had for pregnant
schoolgirls. It was quite a thing.

BAXTER: You must have me confused with someone
else.

JACKIE: You know, I could never understand why
those girls didn't just terminate their pregnancies
and go on with their studies.

BAXTER: Which girls are these?

JACKIE: 'Pudding Club High'.

BAXTER: How long have you known?

JACKIE: The day you arrived. With your bin-bag
of clothes and your harried look of martyrdom.

BAXTER: Well. It was kind of you to pretend
otherwise.

JACKIE: Come on, you knew I knew. Why didn't
they abort and get on with it?

BAXTER: They hated the idea. And having a baby
made them feel grown-up.

JACKIE: At fifteen, sixteen?

BAXTER: Younger.

JACKIE: Stupid.

BAXTER: I don't know. Some of them were quite
bright, really. One girl graduated from uni with
First Class Honours and the Dean's Award.

JACKIE: What did she study?

BAXTER: Hard to say. Madonna Studies, as far as
I can make out. Or maybe it was Kylie.

JACKIE: No such thing.

BAXTER: She sent me a copy of the thesis. 'A Transgressive [Re]reading in Costume and Product Placement' – I think that was the subtitle.

JACKIE: No!

BAXTER: She's probably in politics by now. Always a place in the Labor Party for costume and product placement.

JACKIE: So what was the hook? Christ, it can't have been the money. What drove you?

BAXTER: Oh, I think the media solved that for everybody afterwards, don't you think? Trouser-work, wasn't it? Sex. I was different then.

JACKIE: So it would seem.

BAXTER: So certain I could make a difference. And everyone believed me. Later on, of course, all the talk was about the 'latent perviness' of the impulse. You know, why else would a middle-aged man take such an interest in pregnant fifteen-year-olds?

JACKIE: So why didn't you refute it?

BAXTER: Refute?

JACKIE: I saw you.

BAXTER: You weren't even there!

JACKIE: On that puerile current affairs show.

BAXTER: Didn't take you long to get to that, did it?

JACKIE: Five times. The same question point-blank —
and you stonewalled. It looked terrible.

BAXTER: Looked?

JACKIE: People thought the worst.

BAXTER: You, Jackie. You thought the worst.

JACKIE: Okay, I thought the worst, but you looked
evasive—

BAXTER: Guilty.

JACKIE: Caught out.

BAXTER: Costume and product placement. She was
onto something, that kid.

JACKIE: Oh, very gnomic.

BAXTER: Course I looked caught out, you're meant to look caught out.

JACKIE: You're meant to tell the truth!

BAXTER: It's only television, shipmate, not life itself.

JACKIE: Bullshit.

BAXTER: The news doesn't need to be true, it just needs to be familiar. There's a script.

JACKIE: You were – what – misquoted, misinterpreted, edited? You said nothing. There wasn't much to manipulate.

BAXTER: Except silence.

JACKIE: Evasive.

BAXTER: Can't have silence. Not allowed.

JACKIE: So you clammed up out of sheer perversity?

BAXTER: An unfortunate-sounding word to describe the exercise of a principle.

JACKIE: Upon what grand principle did you employ silence? Why say nothing?

BAXTER: To spare my mother.

JACKIE: This is beautiful.

BAXTER: She was still alive.

JACKIE: So it was mere shame?

BAXTER: I felt I didn't have the right.

JACKIE: To confess?

BAXTER: To explain myself.

JACKIE: You had mitigating circumstances you couldn't speak about in front of your mother.

BAXTER: She was a very private person, fragile.

JACKIE: Everyone thinks their mum's fragile.

BAXTER: She'd endured enough disgrace without me parading it on national telly as a means of defending myself.

JACKIE: But you're her son. The situation you were in, the things people were accusing you of, surely privacy was a luxury she'd forgo. For your sake.

BAXTER: Well, I no longer had the luxury of asking. She had dementia by then. She didn't know who I was anymore.

JACKIE: I'm lost, Baxter. Your mother was non compos but you still couldn't say anything?

BAXTER: Jackie, she raised me on her own. Pregnant at sixteen. No shame in that for me. But she came from a different time. The social disgrace. It was a total bloody catastrophe. She'd had her sights set on teachers' college – big dream for a working-class girl. But . . . enter little Stewie Baxter.

JACKIE: And no wedding.

BAXTER: Grammar school boy. Untouchable. The iron curtain of privilege descends.

JACKIE: So—

BAXTER: So I know what a thwarted life looks like, close up. God bless her, she spared me the sense that I was personally responsible, that I'd ruined her. That's something saintly, if you ask me, it's bloody hard to do. And twenty years later, when I was in my last year at uni, she went back to high school, to live it out, finish what she started.

JACKIE: Good for her.

BAXTER: Yeah, good for her. She got into university.
I felt a kind of spiritual euphoria at the time.
And a week before her first class she had an
asthma attack, clinically dead in the ambulance.
Somehow at Royal Perth they revived her. But
afterwards she sort of went to pieces, as if her
whole personality disintegrated. She became
fearful, insecure, breakdown after breakdown . . .
She was robbed, trapped, stunted. I saw girls
beginning the same journey as hers and I wanted
to spare them. That's all it was. I just didn't have
the . . . luxury of saying so.

JACKIE *gets up to leave. She clambers across to her boat.*

JACKIE: Baxter, I'm sorry.

BAXTER: No, stay. Don't worry about it.

JACKIE: No, you were right. I was indulging myself,
fishing for secrets.

BAXTER: Girl's gotta have one vice left.

Light on JACKIE *as she climbs onto the boom.*

JACKIE: I wasn't the sort of girl my mother hoped
for. And it was cruel. Knowing, watching, feeling

how much it hurt, what it cost her to hide the
disappointment. Wouldn't have occurred to the
old man – disguising his ruined expectations. But
Mum? Mum . . . And there you are – after years
of defiance – just looking for approval. You go on
laying tributes at their feet. Like a cat that finally
brings home a mouse. But she's so far gone in her
disappointment she can't even see you're trying –
it's, it's cruel. God, what a life . . . what a long
improbable journey. Nights like this, it just . . .
it feels like someone else's voyage, not mine. [*She
laughs bitterly*.] I used to know why I was here,
floating in the shadows of the city, tethered but
not tied. At some point it felt decisive – sell the
house, blow off the whole debt-for-dirt thing.
Eventually sinks in: you're alone again and this
time it's for good. Solo, single-handed. So,
embrace it – suck it up, girl, and why not do it
in style? Who can sneer at a beautiful, authentic
wooden boat? No one can quite bring themselves
to hate you for having it. It's not like you're
bobbing about on some white plastic stink boat
like every other try-hard weekend warrior. You're
living their dream. You own it free and clear and
you're living on it. You can feel the grudging
respect. For the first time in your life – well,
since the days when you rode around in a panel
van doing bog-laps with the local small-town
bad boy – you're cool. Cool. What crap, what
a delicious lie you tell yourself: that you've left it

all behind. The girl you were, the woman you've been, the screaming mess you are inside. Because your lovely sloop is just another bit of buoyant gentrification. A husk to hide in. And the real you is hanging on by your breaking nails while the continent presses you out and the sea comes sucking at you like memory. Girt by a sea you could swallow in a moment, you're so desperate.

DEE: [*rising, like a bad thought*] Desperate.

JACKIE: Yes, desperate.

DEE: You fuckin look it.

JACKIE: And there you are, princess, drifting along, smelling of bile and Bacardi, late to the revolution—

DEE: What bloody revolution?

JACKIE: You think you're safe because your skin's perfect.

DEE: [*defiant*] I'm hot, though. You know I am.

JACKIE: Yeah, well, good luck to you. See you in twenty years.

DEE: You won't even know me.

JACKIE: Rest my case.

DEE: 'Cause you'll be so old you won't even know what day it is, Gran.

JACKIE: Ouch.

DEE: Dry as a sucked orange already.

JACKIE: Dry isn't so bad.

DEE: I can feel you looking.

JACKIE: Which is why you're dressed like that.

DEE: My right.

JACKIE: True. So why not look, I tell myself. My right, too. Get over it.

DEE: But I can feel it.

JACKIE: Oh, you're a victim, now.

DEE: Dirty pervy bitch.

JACKIE: You're not safe, Sister, but you're safe from me.

DEE: And I'm tired.

JACKIE: Haven't even started. You've done nothing; you're an infant.

DEE: So sick, tired.

DEE subsides, sleeps. JACKIE *reaches down to caress her but resists at the last moment.*

The dinghy tracks and is gone.

A crash and a sudden light on COL *who wavers drunkenly on the jetty.*

COL: Jesus Christ, you slippery-tongued hypocrite! Here's me thinking it's small-minded busybodies makin ya life a misery, the poor innocent do-gooder just tryin to help out. You had them in the house, for fuck's sake!

JACKIE: Oh God, you've been talking to Ray.

COL *swings aboard* BAXTER'*s boat uninvited.*

COL: And Ruffles and bloody Gilligan there in the Beneteau – Jesus, Jackie, I'd heard things but this—

JACKIE: It was all over the telly—

COL: I haven't got a telly and you bloody know why. He's right here, right in our midst and you never said a word.

JACKIE: And you've trusted me for years for that very reason.

COL: It's not the same! [*to* BAXTER] And you! Couldn't help yourself, you dense prick.

BAXTER: It wasn't like that.

COL: Oh, it's never like that. Not me, Your Honour!

BAXTER: Bugger off, Col. I don't have to justify myself to you.

COL: 'I've paid my debt to society.'

BAXTER: I don't owe any debt.

COL: Only 'cause you didn't get convicted.

BAXTER: Convicted! I wasn't even charged with anything, so go stuff yourself.

COL: Talk to me like that, sonny! I'll crack you one!

JACKIE: Have a lie-down, Col.

COL: Not too old to be put over a man's knee and given a few stripes!

BAXTER: In your dreams, you silly old coot.

COL *lunges at* BAXTER *and they grapple a moment.*

No man. No man ever put me over his knee.

COL: You think I can't see that? You fuckwit!

JACKIE: Oh, for God's sake!

COL *gets him in a headlock.*

COL: It's why you're a dove in a serpent's world, son. No man ever flogged some sense into you. No man ever cared enough. Oh, good Christ!

COL *lets go, doubled up.*

BAXTER: You hurt?

COL: Gotta piss.

BAXTER: The head's blocked.

COL: And that's the least of it. I'll use me own.

JACKIE: Just don't fall in.

COL: Not gunna bloody fall in.

He leaps to his own boat and teeters perilously close to going over.

   [*Glancing back*] Christ, what a disappointment you
     turned out to be. Breaks a man's fuckin heart.

He goes below.

BAXTER: Disappointment!

JACKIE: No wonder he's disappointed. You're like
   a son to him.

BAXTER: Oh, please. A son?

From below, COL*'s howl of urinary agony. The unsavoury tinkle begins, falters, continues.*

You know, I met my father once. Mum's funeral.
   Some kindhearted relative pointed him out.
   By then he was very frail, all one-sided from
   a stroke. I can't tell you the vicious pleasure it
   gave me, seeing him like that. As if the stroke was
   us, me and Mum – his dark secret – suddenly
   taking back our half, getting our due after all
   those years.

JACKIE: What'd you say to him?

BAXTER: Say? Nothing. And you know what, he
looked crestfallen. He was disappointed.

Lights up on the BOY *as he runs, unnoticed along the jetty,
a kite string angling up behind him. He tugs the unseen kite,
laughing, stumbling, hanging on to his hat, and is yanked back
and forth a little himself until, finally, the string goes slack and
instead of the expected kite, a big fish falls from the sky and
thuds onto the jetty. The* BOY *stares at it a while before taking
it in his arms and carrying it off, hugged to his chest.*

Lights up on the boats.

END OF ACT ONE

Dee (Clare Lovering) and Baxter (John Howard)

ACT 2

COL *and* BAXTER *on the deck of the* Shirley.

COL: [*demanding*] Tell me about the girl.

BAXTER: [*gesturing toward* DEE] Nothing to tell, Col, she's still out to it.

COL: Not her. You know who I'm talkin about.

JACKIE *comes out on the deck of the* Mercy.

JACKIE: Col.

COL: He's only been feedin ya half the story, Jackie. Tell us the truth, son.

BAXTER: What difference would it make? I quit, alright? They fired me.

COL: Which was it?

BAXTER: Who cares? I don't remember.

JACKIE: I thought you were forced to quit.

BAXTER: They didn't fire me.

COL: The girl?

BAXTER: Oh, the girl, the girl, the girl!

DEE: [*stirring momentarily*] Sinking. Lemme go.

BAXTER: Jesus, it wasn't just a girl.

COL: Oh, gets better 'n' better, dunnit?

BAXTER: They had nowhere else to go. Look, it was just two kids who wanted to be together. I tried to find somewhere for them, but there was nothing.

JACKIE: Two kids from your school? Students?

BAXTER: Well, she was, yeah.

COL: From the Pudding Club.

BAXTER: Thank you, Col, yes.

JACKIE: So you—

BAXTER: Yes, my place.

JACKIE: And you're living alone. With this couple?
These children.

BAXTER: No, not quite.

COL: Like a bloody eel, isn't he?

BAXTER: I had an old caravan out the back. They
moved in there with the baby. It was only
supposed to be temporary.

COL: Here we go.

BAXTER: It was completely innocent.

COL: Christ, you know as much about life as you do
about boats.

BAXTER: They're out in the van, it's Canning Vale
in February, Jackie, and the bub's fretting and the
kids are getting frayed, so . . . I brought 'em into
the house.

JACKIE: And this girl was supposed to be studying?

BAXTER: Well, best she could manage. You know, without support from the poor shocked family. The parents abandoned her in the first place, kicked her out on the street with no money and a baby – I mean how do you do that, what kind of human can do that? And then they try and crucify me for helping. Always the same story, let the teacher do the work of the parents.

JACKIE: And the boy?

BAXTER: Hip pocket on a singlet. Hated me, the lazy little prick.

JACKIE *and* COL *exchange glances.*

Well, it was awkward.

COL: [*realising*] You fell for her, didn't you?

JACKIE: Oh, Baxter.

BAXTER: The boy bolted.

JACKIE: Left you with the girl, alone.

COL: And he sang like a canary, I'll bet.

BAXTER: Lied his head off. Straight to the girl's parents. They had Tabloid TV on speed dial. Got all interested in her welfare then. Cha-ching!

COL: Dirty old Mister Baxter.

BAXTER: Yeah, the headlines wrote themselves. Hardly required an interview.

JACKIE: Tell me you didn't get involved with that kid.

BAXTER: Involved? Of course I was involved. I'd gone out on a limb for her.

JACKIE: Tell me you didn't have sex with her.

BAXTER: [*affecting an American accent*] I did not have sex with that woman. Okay?

JACKIE: What did you do to make the boy hate you?

BAXTER: Nothing. I was helping the little shit.

COL: People'll forgive you anything but the things you do for 'em.

BAXTER: Says who?

COL: Stalin?

BAXTER *and* JACKIE *can only stare in disbelief.*

JACKIE: You were competing for the girl's affections.

BAXTER: Not consciously, no—

JACKIE: But that was the upshot.

BAXTER: [*almost, by his shrug, admitting this*] I was just trying to do the right thing by the lass. But every kindness on my part, every thing I tried to do for her and the bub made him surly. Ungrateful little prick.

JACKIE: Well, you may have been an old fart in his eyes, Baxter, but you did have a job and a house and money . . .

BAXTER: Look, I know this now, don't I—?

JACKIE: And what was he? A penniless, pimply sixteen-year-old. So the more you helped his girlfriend the more hopeless he became—

BAXTER: [*exasperated*] Oh! Ridiculous.

JACKIE: And it must have been humiliating for him.

BAXTER: Oh, the poor love. Only got the lass pregnant. But what about me? I didn't do anything wrong.

COL: The principled principal.

BAXTER: I still can't believe the pettiness of it.

JACKIE: Really? You think it wasn't a mistake?

BAXTER: A strategic error, but not anything wrong.

JACKIE: God, where does this sense of moral immunity come from?

COL: Start with the teachers' union, love, and work back.

BAXTER: I didn't do it – what they said, what was implied.

COL: Implied? Christ, son . . . [*Gesturing at the entire marina*] They're all pissed and talking; it's like fire along the jetty and here's me like a halfwit tryin to douse the flames. But they've all got you pegged as a kiddy fiddler!

DEE *sits up on deck, disoriented, waking slowly, unnoticed. The slur hangs in the air.*

BAXTER: Thank you for that, Col.

JACKIE: And you deny it?

BAXTER: Of course I bloody deny it, because it never happened!

COL: Wasn't she a looker? Weren't you tempted?

JACKIE: Jesus, Col.

COL: Just askin. It's all old rope to me. Can't even piss straight.

BAXTER: You want me to describe her? Is this what it's about, Jackie? You want a bit of a voyeuristic hand rub like Col here?

COL: [*simultaneous*] Hey, hey!

JACKIE: [*simultaneous*] How dare you!

BAXTER: She was blonde, Jackie, dirty dishwater blonde. Blue eyes, pouty mouth. Her breasts were still tight with milk—

JACKIE: I can't believe I'm hearing this—

COL: [*too eager by half*] And?

BAXTER: And when she came out of the shower, wrapped in towels, she smelled like something freshly baked.

COL: Freshly baked?

BAXTER: Britney Keene.

COL: Eyes of blue and knees obscene.

BAXTER: Of course I was fucking tempted. I didn't do what they said, but I'd be a liar if I told you the thought never crossed my mind.

JACKIE: [*attempting to quell her fury*] And what was she thinking, you reckon?

BAXTER: I couldn't begin to say.

JACKIE: You don't imagine she ever felt the pressure to repay your kindness with . . . favours?

BAXTER: The only favours that girl ever offered me were fish fingers and oven-fried chips. Otherwise she did her very best not to leave shitty nappies on the kitchen bench, or female hygienic appliances in the bathroom. But I have no idea what she was thinking. Christ, I can barely make out what I was thinking.

JACKIE: Maybe you weren't thinking at all.

COL: Thinkin with his knob.

BAXTER: Get stuffed.

COL: Oh, you'd set your mind on higher things, no doubt.

BAXTER: Yes, actually. Which may have been a mistake, I'll admit it. For some reason, once the 'news broke' I decided to tough it out, carry on as if I was safe up there in the broad sunshine of the high moral ground. I'm telling myself: the Ed Department, the media, the bolshie parent groups, the purveyors of moral panic – how can they hurt us if I'm doing nothing wrong?

COL: Talk about into the shit storm without a brolly.

JACKIE: But in the end—

BAXTER: The beginning was my end. I was toast, a puff of blue smoke, Jackie.

Silence.

JACKIE: And the girl, she stuck up for you?

BAXTER *gives her a wry glance to disabuse her.*

> COL: Nice cheque from the telly people, I spose.
> Call it a baby bonus.

> BAXTER: Well, she didn't exactly tell any lies.

> COL: But.

> BAXTER: Given how things proceeded, the financial
> rewards and the celebrity of the moment . . . it
> seems it wasn't in her immediate interests to tell
> the whole truth.

> COL: You fuckwit.

> BAXTER: Indeed.

> COL: You didn't even touch her?

> BAXTER: Oh, I had to have touched her in passing,
> helping her with the baby, in the kitchen—

> COL: You know that's not what I mean!

> BAXTER: There was no inappropriate touching, Col.
> Sorry to disappoint you again.

COL *absorbs this news and is placated.* DEE *watches and
listens surreptitiously.*

COL: Hm. Man can't shit or blow his nose these days without worrying how it looks.

JACKIE: Having a sixteen-year-old breastfeeding student in the home of an unmarried headmaster is a little more complicated than the business of defecation, Col—

COL: Defecation, libel, it's all the same to me.

JACKIE: Yes, I'm beginning to see how it would be.

BAXTER: You know, sometimes I wonder why I didn't try my luck with her.

JACKIE: Oh, please!

BAXTER: I was damned anyway; I might as well have gone ahead and done it – the consequences would have been the same.

JACKIE: That's bullshit and you know it.

BAXTER: And I might have had some slimy satisfaction to compensate for all the shame and innuendo.

JACKIE: I don't need to hear this—

BAXTER: But you love a secret, Jackie. You picked the scab, shipmate, and now you're squeamish about the pus? The truth is I do sometimes think I was a bit of a coward.

JACKIE: Enough!

BAXTER: You've got all the answers, Jackie – was I teaching all those years for power? You don't have to be any kind of genius to be a teacher, or even much of a grown-up. You just need to be a week ahead of the class. Everyone else in the room is poorer, weaker, less experienced and maybe you get to like that. All those pretty, pliant young things, upturned heads, curling eyelashes.

JACKIE: Is that all it was? Is that who you are?

An almighty explosion introduces the fireworks display that flickers and flashes mostly out of view across the harbour. COL and BAXTER climb up onto the jetty for a better view. JACKIE stays aboard the Mercy, *and on the* Shirley DEE *rises, rummages in her pack a while before creeping below. She's gone a while and the BOY rows into view, taking in the fireworks, a rod trolling a line behind him. He sees DEE stagger back on deck and vomit over the transom, soiling her crop-top in the process. She recovers herself and takes a bucket with a rope attached to haul up some seawater, and the BOY watches as she sluices herself. Nobody sees it but him. DEE wrings out her top, sniffs at it doubtfully. The BOY gets a bite and his attention is wrenched away. He fights the line and is towed to and fro across the water as the fireworks crack and whistle and fizz above him. Finally, after a great struggle, he hauls in a kite. With one final shell burst he's gone.*

Light on COL *and* BAXTER *as they stand a moment on the jetty, still staring up at the night sky. They swing back aboard their vessels.*

COL: How's that, eh? Better'n sex.

BAXTER: And as an annual event, so much more frequent.

JACKIE: [*seeing* DEE] Oh. Look who's with us.

BAXTER: [*to* DEE] You alright there?

DEE *nods.*

JACKIE: But you're wet through.

DEE: I'm okay. All good.

JACKIE: [*to* BAXTER] Listen, I've gotta go. I was supposed to be in town half an hour ago.
[*To* DEE] You need a lift somewhere?

COL: In the Karmann Ghia. Never offers me a ride in it.

DEE: No. Not right now.

BAXTER: A shirt, Jackie. A blouse?

JACKIE: Give her one of yours. You know, the way
a bloke always will.

BAXTER: Yeah, thanks.

JACKIE *leaves, texting as she goes.*

DEE: Bitch.

COL *looks with lascivious interest at her breasts in the wet
singlet.* JACKIE *sees it but goes inside again for her phone and
keys.* BAXTER *begins to tidy up nervously. He tries to ignore
the broad winks from* COL.

COL: I've just gotta go below and fix the weasel
gasket on the crapulator. Needs adjustment.
Might be a little while.

BAXTER: There's no need, Col.

COL: Nah, dicky business, the weasel gasket. Might
have ya hands full, eh?

BAXTER: Whatever you reckon, Col.

COL *goes below.*

[*To* DEE] What about a walk? Clear your head.

DEE *shakes her head.*

There's some food here.

DEE *declines vehemently without a word.*

Maybe a ginger beer?

DEE, *in the grip of a rolling nausea, is unable to respond.*
BAXTER *goes below and returns with a shirt and a bottle of*
ginger beer.

It's warm, I'm afraid. The ginger beer, I mean.

DEE *takes the shirt from him and he turns away ostentatiously*
as she peels off her singlet and pulls on his ridiculous 'G'DAY
WA' shirt.

Here, it'll settle your tummy.

DEE: [*derisively*] My tummy.

She takes it anyway, but has barely put it to her lips before she's
heaving over the side. A hatch moves on COL's *boat and it's*
obvious he's watching.

Aw, fuck! Fuckin hell. Fuckin fuck.

BAXTER *begins to speak but is stopped by another of* DEE*'s spasms. He tries again, several times, only to be cut off by heaves, half-heaves, phantom heaves and then a hiccup. Finally he concedes defeat and retreats to where* DEE*'s rucksack lies on the deck. He stoops to pick it up.*

Don't you bloody touch it.

BAXTER: But I—

DEE: I don't care. You don't touch it.

BAXTER: I'll just move it out of the way.

DEE: No. Thievin bastards.

BAXTER: I can assure you—

DEE: Don't try assurin me of nuffing, mate. I'm past bein assured.

BAXTER *shuffles the pack aside with his foot and comes back to peer at* DEE*'s head. She cowers a little, despite herself.*

BAXTER: We should put some antiseptic on that.

DEE: I'm fine, yeah?

BAXTER: Where you from?

DEE: You have to ask?

BAXTER: I mean, where in the UK?

DEE: London. Heard of it?

BAXTER: Where in London?

DEE: North Four. Finsbury Park.

BAXTER: Ha. I was there once.

DEE: What for, the Battle of Britain?

BAXTER: 1979. Thatcher and everything. Don't
suppose you were even born.

DEE: Not even close.

BAXTER: Hm, Finsbury Park.

DEE: Believe me, you wouldn't know it.

BAXTER: Imagine it's changed.

DEE: Don't even think about it. It'd make you sick
to your stomach. [*A beat as she realises what she's
said.*] How much is a cab to the airport?

BAXTER: Forty, fifty bucks, I spose, maybe more. Heading out?

DEE: I'm over it.

BAXTER: Ah.

DEE: And I don't have fifty dollars.

BAXTER *ponders this a moment before remembering his crab pot. He pulls it in and shakes two crabs into a bucket.*

BAXTER: How's that for competition? One's eaten the other's legs off. Fighting over a hunk of spleen.

DEE: Yeah, that's the spirit.

BAXTER: Quite the modern creature, our crab. One for the Productivity Commission.

DEE: Ha-bloody-ha.

BAXTER: You've got a ticket, still? And a passport?

DEE: Yes, Dad, but I need fifty bucks.

BAXTER: Why would Finsbury Park make me sick to my stomach?

DEE: Maybe it wouldn't. Maybe you're a raghead.

BAXTER: A what?

DEE: You got no idea.

BAXTER: So I gather.

DEE: Think sandals, mate. Beards, bombs, backpacks, burqas. Street full of Pakis kowtowin to Mecca.

BAXTER: Ah.

DEE: Is it true, then, about you being a kiddy fiddler?

BAXTER: What?

DEE: A nonce; I heard youse talking.

BAXTER: Well, you heard wrong. You're drunk.

DEE: Drunk and broke, yeah. Not deaf.

BAXTER: You heard wrong.

DEE: That right?

BAXTER: Listen, get some rest, sleep it off.

DEE: I need fifty dollars.

BAXTER: We'll talk about it in the morning.

DEE: Yes, Dad. Right you are then, Dad. Dear old
Dad. Shame he's a nonce, innit?

BAXTER: Cut it out.

DEE: Oooh, all narky now.

BAXTER: Not at all.

DEE: Don't blame me, Sir. You said it, Sir. I heard
you, Sir.

BAXTER: I said nothing of the sort.

DEE: Said you bloody wished you had.

BAXTER: That'll do.

DEE: In for a penny, in for a pound. Those milky
little tits, I bet. That's what did it. And no one
even there to see it but the baby.

BAXTER: I said that's enough.

DEE: She did it for Daddy.

BAXTER: Shut your mouth.

DEE: Or what? You'll lay hands on me? Ooh,
    constable!

BAXTER: No. But you can get the hell off my boat.

DEE: Then what'll I do?

BAXTER: That's your problem.

DEE: No, it's your problem, 'cause I got a loud
    voice. Bit unladylike. Liable to wander up and
    down, I am.

A SEAGOING GENTLEMAN, *in white shorts and deck shoes,
heads out along the jetty.*

One boat after the other, telling people what you
    are. Lots more jetties than just this one. Hello,
    sailor!

The SEAGOING GENTLEMAN *hesitates, alerted.* BAXTER
*stares at her in horror, rage, disbelief. She laughs at him. The
interloper clambers over the mast and heads offstage, with
a backward glance.*

Fucking thin-skinned, you.

BAXTER: Jackie's right, I'm an idiot.

DEE: What happened to that girl with the baby. She finish school?

BAXTER: No.

DEE: Go on to be a doctor, did she? Got a fella, has she?

BAXTER: I don't know.

DEE: Another kid? Maybe two? Black eye and a pushchair down the high street?

BAXTER: Possibly. I wouldn't know.

DEE: You've guessed, though, done the odds.

BAXTER: Yes.

DEE: What's her chances? Now the telly money's run out.

BAXTER: Poor.

DEE: Weren't much help, then, were you?

BAXTER: Listen—

DEE: Wasted your time, mate. You were always wasting your time. You can't help 'em. People like you only ever make it worse. Think you're all fucking superheroes!

Roused by the noise, COL *comes up on deck.*

COL: Everything orright over there?

DEE: He's telling me all about himself.

COL: Maybe you should go, love.

DEE: And maybe you should mind your own sodding business.

BAXTER: It's okay, Col; she's pissed.

COL: Yeah, and that's the good news.

BAXTER: Your boyfriend's family. You've got their number? I could call them.

DEE: They don't like me.

COL: And she seems like such a lovely girl.

DEE: Course, they won't say it, but you know why they emigrated?

COL: To escape you, love.

DEE: Not allowed to say it. Don't sound nice.
    Not in front of the new neighbours. Though
    I dunno why they're so careful, mostly other
    Brits, anyroad. They all know – it's the unspoken
    secret. They're not here just for the mine jobs and
    the sunshine. It's not just the fake villa and the
    three-car garage and the SUV and the roll-out
    lawn and the white, sandy beach and baby-blue
    sky and the long pissy lunches.

COL: Christ, she makes it sound like the eighties.
    I'm getting a lump in me throat.

DEE: It's all the white faces.

BAXTER: Love, there's an unprecedented mining
    boom, a labour shortage—

DEE: Proper people, you pillocks!

BAXTER: Proper?

DEE: They're moving here 'cause they feel safe,
    'cause they're surrounded by white people.
    Sydney, Melbourne, nah, it's all Pakis and
    Chinks and Hajjis.

COL: What?

DEE: But drive across the desert in your Wicked van and there's Perth – fucking heaven on a stick. Tell me, is there anywhere, anywhere else in the world as white as this?

COL: Let's call a spade a spade. You're whiter than any of us! I mean we've got our fair share of—

BAXTER: Col—

COL: You callin us racists?

DEE: Have you ever seen a town so waxed and polished and pastel and pasteurised – like a beautiful, cold pint of milk – so tidy and safe . . . do you even see it? Christ, have you driven up through those endless fucking suburbs in your own town, yeah, seen the driveways and letterboxes and lawns? It's a fantasy, it's social pornography, you can hardly believe it's true! Paradise.

COL: Too fucking right!

DEE: It's simple: no Pakis. Yeah? Whiteness. That's why they're here. Read my lips.

COL: There's puke on 'em, love.

DEE: And there's Clive and Nancy up there—

COL: Who?

DEE: Bangin on all afternoon about Dullsville. Moanin like—

COL: Poms.

DEE: The freeway's always gridlocked, never enough buses, can't find a taxi, shops're never open, no smoking this, wear your bicycle helmet that – Christ, you should hear it – but really they fuckin love it. Fat and tanned and livin the life. Twelve thousand miles from Finsbury Park Mosque, they are, in a country where everything's sorted.

BAXTER: Let me get this straight. You told them this? Today?

DEE: [*with a laugh*] At the big barbecue! Let 'em have it.

COL: On Australia Day.

DEE: Out by the pool, all the neighbours and the geezers from work and tennis and Pilates.

COL: Jesus. The fucking arrogance!

DEE: Under the cabana, hot as hell, eatin grilled soddin vegetables with Alfie and Margie and

[*in her ghastly Afrikaner accent*] Hansie and
Frickie and Lucy and Tenille, or whatever, pack
of thin-skinned hypocrites they turned out.

BAXTER: That tattoo of yours.

DEE: I just said what's true, what they all know,
even the *jaapies*.

BAXTER: Yarpies?

COL: South Africans.

DEE: Especially the *jaapies*.

COL: Got their fireworks early, I reckon. Bloody
hell.

DEE: Never said it was right, never said it was nice,
either. But it's bloody true, innit?

COL: Never heard so much shit in all my life.

DEE: You're made of shit, you old wanker! You smell
of piss! Your prostate's bigger than your fucking
brain!

COL: Dirty, pommy slut! [*To* BAXTER] Thanks for
backing a fella up. [*He reels away.*] Dear fucking
diary.

COL *goes below.* DEE *gloats at having seen him off.*

BAXTER: 'Pogrom'. The tattoo. What does it mean?

DEE: What?

BAXTER: Pogrom.

DEE: It's a band. Sir.

BAXTER: A rock band?

DEE: No, a Salvation Army band.

BAXTER: Pogrom.

DEE: They broke up anyway.

BAXTER: Oh.

DEE: Nothing lasts. Nothing good. I need
    a hundred bucks.

BAXTER: A hundred?

DEE: There's the cab at the other end.

BAXTER: What about the Tube?

DEE: Mister World Traveller, 1979. The Tube.

BAXTER: But a hundred dollars . . .

DEE: I'll do the necessary. I don't care. I know what you want.

BAXTER: What I want? What I want?

DEE: Within reason, yeah, nothing nasty.

BAXTER: I don't believe this.

DEE: Here I am, real as life. To Sir with love. And a receipt, if you need it. Keep the VAT man happy. Only plastic Aussie dollars, anyroad.

BAXTER *gets her by the arm. She pulls away, falls to the deck.*

BAXTER: Get up.

DEE: Make me.

BAXTER: C'mon, off the boat.

DEE: Don't get all offended, Sir. You're not that noble. Just a coward. No bottle.

BAXTER: Please.

DEE: All your talk, all your worthy notions. Captain, my Captain. Gar. Just a knob-ache like

all the others. What's a bloke but a cock with
a bad conscience? Your Pudding Prefect – think
she had any more respect for you than she had
for the Welfare and the dole office? You're a pit
stop, mate, an opportunity to use, something to
exploit. Be honest. Just take what you want and
spare us all the tears and the righteous agony. Just
pretend I'm a pudgy little nursing mother with
one tit out. Col can flip himself quietly below
decks. But for you it's cracker night, long as you
don't take it personal. It's all good if you don't let
yourself take it personal.

BAXTER: But I do. Taking things 'personal' is all
that's left.

DEE: You're old. Get over it.

BAXTER: But you're right about one thing.
Sometimes it's best to declare yourself from the
outset, from sheer self-interest, self-preservation.
To get what you want. Which is why I'm telling
you to get the hell off my boat.

DEE: And what if I start screaming?

BAXTER: I'll live with it. Besides, it's a party out
there, everyone's screaming. You'll be just another
pissed idiot. C'mon.

DEE: Tempted, though, aren't you?

BAXTER: Jesus, don't you have any morals, any sense
of personal safety?

DEE: Can't decide if you want to fuck me or save
me, yeah?

BAXTER: They all know about me now. I'm not
afraid of you.

DEE: You poor old bastard, you hardly even exist.

BAXTER: So there goes your hundred bucks.

*He pulls her up roughly and she begins to laugh. He shoves her
toward her pack and she slaps him away and heaves it up onto
the jetty.*

Go.

DEE: I'm going.

She climbs unsteadily up onto the jetty.

Hope you get cancer.

*She straps her pack on, teeters a moment and is gone. A sudden
cry and a splash.*

BAXTER: Jesus! Col!

COL: What? Oh, good Christ!

Blackout.

BAXTER *and* COL*'s voices amid watery confusion.*

BAXTER: Here, here, get a boathook!

COL: I can't see! Jesus, son!

BAXTER: Here, here!

COL: Go!

Lights up to an aquamarine haze where, suspended above the boats and the jetty, DEE *sinks slowly backwards under the weight of her pack, struggling at first and then surrendering.*

The BOY *swims into her field of light and tries to haul her upward, but she's too heavy. She touches the* BOY*'s face.*

DEE: If I sleep, when I sleep, when it's safe, the whole world is like me. And everybody wants me, everybody loves me, they keep me safe, she keeps me safe, and everybody loves me when I sleep. But when you wake you have to fight and scream and scratch for what's left, and none of them can see how little they've left us, so you

fight when really you just want to sleep. Really,
you just want to sleep – for good, forever.

The BOY *tries to rescue the doll, but* DEE's *grip is too strong
and he runs out of breath, swims up and out of view. Light
flickers, fades around* DEE *and there are muted voices above as
it fades away to darkness.*

[*Unseen*] Can't you see it, Mum? I'm here. Can't you
even see me?

The sound of a crashing wave.

Light on the deck of BAXTER's *boat, where* COL *is tipping
water from* DEE's *rucksack. He sets it down before unzipping
it to peer in. He pulls out a sodden magazine, a rancid t-shirt,
a phone. He's still shaking water from it when* BAXTER *comes
up on deck with a towel around his neck and bunch of wet
clothes in his hands.*

COL: [*of the phone*] Cactus. Looking for the passport
and a ticket.

BAXTER: Can't it wait?

COL: Well, you ask yourself.

BAXTER: It can wait.

COL: She asleep?

BAXTER *nods, begins to wring water from the jeans, the t-shirt.*

Thank Christ. I think I prefer it when you drag up a shoppin trolley.

BAXTER: She'll be gone in the morning. It'll be different when she's sober.

COL: Don't get your hopes up, son, and for pity's sake hide your wallet. Geez, she went down like a bag of cats.

BAXTER: She did. Man, that was lucky.

COL: Shoulda left her there.

He watches idly until he realises that they are DEE*'s clothes that* BAXTER *is hanging out.*

You mean to tell me . . . you undressed her? She's down there on your bunk . . . naked?

BAXTER: Don't even think about it, Col.

COL: What, it's only okay for you, is it?

BAXTER: I didn't want her soaking everything, did I? She can't sleep down there in wet clothes. And no, she's not naked, so don't get your feathers up.

COL: Yeah, mate, whatever you reckon.

BAXTER: If Jackie'd been here I would've got her to do it.

COL: And how would that have been any different?

BAXTER: You can't go down there and gawk at her.

COL: Why, isn't it worth it?

BAXTER: Don't be a creep.

COL: You can talk.

BAXTER: Just stop it, alright?

COL *surrenders and climbs across to his own boat. He finds a beer and opens it.*

You weren't serious, were you?

COL: [*with a belch*] Nah. Nah . . . Nah.

BAXTER: I'll sleep up here tonight.

COL: Don't do it on my account.

BAXTER: Hot as hell anyway.

COL: Can't trust anyone these days.

BAXTER: Well, you have to, don't you? Eventually?

COL: Quicksand. It's our nature.

BAXTER: No.

COL: Christ, where've you been? Haven't you learnt anything? You can't trust anyone, not even yourself.

BAXTER: But I'm not the one talking about ducking below for a quick peep, am I?

COL: Ah, it was just talk. A sailor gets lonely.

BAXTER: I thought you had a girl in every port.

COL: What port? This is the only port I've ever been in.

BAXTER: How could you have been in the merchant marine if this is the only port you've been in?

COL: Who says I was in the merchant marine?

BAXTER: Navy, whatever.

COL: I was never in the friggin navy. Who you been talkin to?

BAXTER: You . . . you're always talking about battle
    scars, and the day you scuttled the good ship
    Vigilant.

COL: Vigilant? You clot, Vigilant was a bank.

BAXTER: That Vigilant?

COL: I was an accountant, son. A bean counter.
    For the big—

BAXTER: So, the battle scars—

COL *suddenly tears off his shirt to brandish the marks on
his chest.*

Shit.

COL: Quadruple bypass. Look like a hot crossed
    bun.

BAXTER: I had no idea.

COL: Well . . .

BAXTER: What'd it feel like?

COL: Like I'd been shot. Like I'd been hunted down
    and shot. By God – and the shareholders of nine
    companies.

BAXTER: So, sailing away, throwing off the lines, that's just talk.

COL: Yeah-nah, that's real!

BAXTER: Madagascar? The Cape of Good Hope?

COL: Valparaiso, my oath.

BAXTER: And your family?

COL: Well, you know what they say: where there's a Will, there's relatives. See you in the morning.

BAXTER: You're not staying up? See off the national day?

COL: Nah, I'm gone. Went too hard too early. Whoop it up without me.

BAXTER: Good night, then.

Party sounds fade until only the lap of water and the groan of ropes and the whinny of shackles remain. BAXTER sits motionless with his thoughts. Falls asleep. Eventually a new set of footsteps rings down the boardwalk. JACKIE comes out along the jetty, hesitates at her own boat, watching BAXTER doze. She takes the few extra steps to draw alongside his boat.

JACKIE: Permission to come aboard.

BAXTER: Oh! Jackie. Yeah.

JACKIE *kicks off her heels and swings down.*

JACKIE: You asleep?

BAXTER: No. Course not. You look cheerful.

JACKIE: Some bloke gave me a bag of mangoes.
    On the street. Just like that. Want one?

She surveys all the hanging laundry and notes DEE*'s things
hanging in the rigging.*

Looks like a Bangkok slum down here.

BAXTER: Did you know Col was an accountant?

JACKIE: M-hm.

BAXTER: Any idea who he worked for? He's all
    skittish about it.

JACKIE: Understandable. In the circumstances.

BAXTER: You know, then?

JACKIE: Bits and pieces.

BAXTER: And?

JACKIE: He'd rather not discuss it.

BAXTER: You mean you won't tell me?

JACKIE: He asked me never to tell. You know how Perth works, Baxter. Same old faces, same old fingers in the till.

BAXTER: So why'd he tell you?

JACKIE: Why indeed? Perhaps he wasn't in a fit state. And maybe my being a woman meant that it didn't really count.

BAXTER: Must have counted for something if he asked you never to tell. Maybe he trusts you.

JACKIE: He may not even remember.

BAXTER: So what's the harm in telling?

JACKIE: Because I'd know I betrayed him even if he didn't.

BAXTER: Then he's a better judge of character than he knows. Must really be something, something to keep quiet about.

JACKIE: You know how it is, one big, happy family out here in the west.

BAXTER: And Col knows where all the bodies are buried. The eighties? Come on, indulge me.

JACKIE: I'm always indulging you. Both of you. It's my neighbourly workout.

BAXTER: I've seen you some mornings. Meditating.

JACKIE: Oh, yeah?

BAXTER: Does it help?

JACKIE: With being neighbourly, yes.

BAXTER: I meant with your . . . challenges, your demons.

JACKIE: My demons.

BAXTER: God, you're inscrutable. It's impressive, don't get me wrong, but it's a little intimidating. Don't you ever let go?

JACKIE: Only if I'm a mess. And I don't want to be that kind of mess again. Ever. I do my own accounting, I face my own shit. I have an addiction. I don't care for endless iteration.

BAXTER: But you went to a meeting tonight.

JACKIE: And?

BAXTER: AA. Right?

JACKIE: That's maintenance, not confession.

BAXTER: Why tonight?

JACKIE: Had my reasons.

BAXTER: And here we are, all of us, pissed and
unlovely. It must set you off.

JACKIE: Don't flatter yourself. It's an anniversary.
A personal thing, a private thing.

BAXTER: At a meeting like that, doesn't everyone
share?

JACKIE: If it's useful. I'll listen if someone needs
to be heard.

BAXTER: Or can be made to spill the beans.

JACKIE: You wanted to, Baxter.

BAXTER: Which is how you justify it to yourself.
You satisfied your curiosity.

JACKIE: I needed to know.

BAXTER: But until now you didn't need to, all these months it was hear no evil.

JACKIE: Yes, I'm sorry – suddenly I did. Baxter, you live an arm's length away. And I'm jetlagged and fed up and I realise it's today, this day, and then, as if that isn't enough suddenly there's this . . . child [*pointing below*] turning up. And there's you, and your little challenges. And I'm worried. I'm thinking, is this actually about to happen in front of me, the sort of thing people are talking about? I needed to know.

BAXTER: And what about what I need to know? About you.

JACKIE: I'm not talking domestic detail, you moron, I mean character. You already know enough about mine to make a judgement. What I did in a state of intoxication in another life isn't relevant here.

BAXTER: Perhaps you're right.

JACKIE: Do try to sound sincere.

BAXTER: Sorry.

JACKIE: Look: I had a friend when we were kids, just country bogans. He was a simple person, but a complicated sort of friend – no one in town quite like him. For a long time I thought I loved him. But in the end . . . I just wasn't a friend. I wasn't loyal. They destroyed him. And now he's dead. The rest of my sad little journey is just petty heartache, Baxter, loves that didn't work out. Maybe one day I'll bore you with those amusing details, but him I don't need to talk about; in fact I need to not talk about it. I can't outrun it. I just need to outlive it.

BAXTER: What was his name?

JACKIE *sighs*.

You can't say it. It'll kill you.

JACKIE *retreats to the transom*.

You think you're at the mercy of everything you've done?

JACKIE: Everything you've ever given off is already out there, yes, in the atmosphere, soil, rivers, sea, it stays in your body somehow, in your water, and your memory, every tic and habit, accumulating—

BAXTER: Metastasising.

JACKIE: It's just there, always.

BAXTER: And there's nothing we can do to stop it, this collision with the past?

JACKIE: I don't know.

BAXTER: Storm, pestilence?

JACKIE: You're the geography teacher.

BAXTER: I'm nothing.

JACKIE: Don't be ridiculous.

BAXTER: No, it suits me. Happy to be nothing. It's a relief.

JACKIE: Nature needs a storm, a bit of chaos. Maybe we do too.

BAXTER: You've thought about this?

JACKIE: Only in the mornings and afternoons.

BAXTER: So, then it's hopeless? Everything behind us is just grinding us forward to disaster?

JACKIE: No. I can't think like that. Won't live like that.

BAXTER: What, in the face of oblivion you've decided to look on the bright side?

JACKIE: I look for courage.

BAXTER: On the sunny side of the street.

JACKIE: There is no sunny side.

BAXTER: Exactly.

JACKIE: I've seen your toy noose. Life's fucked, the planet's doomed, off you go.

BAXTER: You ruthless bastard.

JACKIE: Life's tough. And you're disappointed in yourself. I understand. Boo-hoo. Here's fifty bucks, buy a ladder and get over yourself.

BAXTER: But, Jackie, you can't live by force of will.

JACKIE: No. But you have to leave the hatch open for the breeze. Even if, in your heart, you feel as if the air will never stir again. It's not much, I know, but it's how I get through the day. Hoping change is possible, not really expecting it.

BAXTER: Christ, Jack, you're an Amazon, a warrior.

JACKIE: Baxter, your suffering's real enough. It's just that in the scheme of things, in the universe of suffering, it isn't very special.

BAXTER: Ow. Undistinguished, even in my anguish.

JACKIE: See you in the morning. I want to get to sleep before the flotilla finds its way back downriver. I assume you still have company?

BAXTER: [*gesturing below*] She went for a swim. Sleeping it off.

JACKIE: Convenient.

BAXTER: I'll be up on deck, don't worry.

JACKIE: Now why would I worry?

BAXTER: Hey. Pogrom.

JACKIE: What?

BAXTER: Pogrom. Apparently it's a band.

JACKIE: Ah.

BAXTER: They've broken up.

JACKIE: See? Good things never last.

BAXTER: But look on the bright side, eh?

JACKIE: [*before she goes below*] You'll be alright?

BAXTER: Meaning, can I be trusted to do the babysitting?

JACKIE: Meaning, will you be alright?

BAXTER: Scout's honour. I'll be flying the flag for the rest of you.

Blackout.

The sounds of returning diesels, muffled curses, bagged bottles and a ragged chorus of jingoistic anthems that fades until the faint sounds of the sleeping harbour city resume.

A light on the BOY *who rows silently across the water. When he reaches* BAXTER'S *boat he makes fast to it and climbs nimbly aboard.* BAXTER *sleeps on. The* BOY *picks up cans, sniffs leftover food, and examines the clothes and artifacts strung up in the rigging. When he comes upon the hangman's noose he looks at* BAXTER *through the portal of its bight. As he squats beside the sleeping* BAXTER *he unties the knot and coils the rope over and over in his hands.* BAXTER *stirs briefly but sleeps on.*

BOY: Some nights, out in the sleepout, I lie awake
and listen to the long, green sound of the night.
You know, if you listen hard, if you hold your
breath, you can hear behind all the other tiny
sounds. There's a warm, quiet roar, like the
faintest sound of the sea inside a shell. In a shell
it's not really the sea you're hearing. Well, not
just the sea. It's the sky, too, and the ground
underneath, the earth-sound coming up the
stumps of the house. It's in the bones of your
ears, the taste on your tongue. You know when
you sleep it'll go on around you, keep going,
green and quiet under the eaves, in the trees,
along the street.

*Below decks the sound of a woman weeping. Then another. It
goes on faintly while the* BOY *listens. He climbs up into the
rigging and squats like a nightbird on a spar.*

Some nights I hear her. My mum. Weeping. Trying
to do it quiet, like she thinks I won't hear. I want
to go in there and say something, hold her, climb
in beside her, but I know I'm not supposed to –
it'll only make things worse. It's hard being
alone. I lie there, wait and wait and wait till she
stops and she's all worn out with it, and all I can
do is hope that when it's finished she'll hear the
green sound, that little, thin, hollow noise of the
world alive, before she goes to sleep.

A light on DEE *who emerges from below, wrapped in a sheet. She wipes tears from her face and looks at* BAXTER *sleeping on deck. The marina is still, the city sleeps. The* BOY *watches.*

DEE: Gap year. If you have a good enough time you won't remember a thing. You want to forget yourself, suddenly remember a new you. Not the spineless you, not the bullshit you. Know what I mean? Sir? Mister Chalk, Sir? The you that stays and fights. Sticks it out.

BAXTER *stirs and mumbles, but does not wake.*

Sposed to be the two of us, Lexie and me. Girls going ga-ga. Thailand, Cambodia, the whole disaster. But in Vietnam there's this orphanage. AIDS kids, mostly. And Lexie gets all . . . well, we both did. Me, it lasted three days, tops. Like, they're so cute, and small, sound like little birds. Want to touch your hair, hold you. It's great, your heart, your heart . . . But it's so hot and everything stinks and you know you're, like, 'There'll always be more orphans, you can't really make a difference, it's soft, thinking you can . . . '

She begins to gather her damp clothes, to dress, and to assemble her things as BAXTER *snores on.*

And mates are messaging from Bali and Sydney, and . . . well, I bunked off. Middle of the night.

How's that for loyal? Best friends forever. Such
a good place to hate yourself in, this, isn't it, Sir?
Well, maybe I owe you something, owe meself.
Do you a favour.

Dressed and ready to leave, DEE *goes below. The* BOY *watches,
fascinated. Sounds of rummaging. The squeak of a tap,
another; water pouring.* DEE *reappears. She stoops to wash her
face from the bucket but gasps and recoils, and* BAXTER *wakes.*

BAXTER: Mind your fingers.

DEE: Bloody crabs.

BAXTER: You're off then?

She nods. BAXTER *fishes in his pocket. He hands her some
money.*

DEE: Forty dollars.

BAXTER: Sorry. It's all I've got on me.

DEE: Thanks anyway. I'll pay it back.

BAXTER: Yeah.

DEE: And thanks for fishing me out. Really.
I would've drowned.

BAXTER: Maybe. Probably.

She extends a hand and they shake.

DEE: You're a trip.

She fishes in her pocket.

BAXTER: Same to you.

DEE: [*handing him his watch and phone*] And you better have these back.

BAXTER: Ah. Well. Safe journey home, eh?

DEE: Home?

BAXTER: Well, wherever it is you're going.

DEE: Right, yeah. What about you? Where are you sailing?

BAXTER: Oh, trails to adventure, me. Nah, I'm not goin anywhere. I'm set.

DEE: Well, you never know. Learn quick when you need to.

She climbs up onto the jetty and looks back a moment.

You should get out more.

BAXTER: So I'm told. You'll be alright?

DEE: Yeah. It's all good. Listen, one thing: can you
swim?

BAXTER: You've got a short memory, anyway I'm an
Australian male: we swim before we can think.

DEE: I believe you. So it's all good, then. You'll be
okay. Don't worry, you'll thank me.

BAXTER: Oh, no doubt. Forty dollars the poorer.

He sits, becalmed and bemused, as DEE *exits hurriedly along
the jetty. He settles back, draws the sarong around him.*

All good, 24/7. Yeah. Back to normal. Thank God.

He gives in to sleep. The BOY *surveys the harbour, the sleeper
below, as the gurgle of water gains pace.*

BOY: I like the smell of sunshine in my pillow. I like
the secret skin, that smooth square behind a girl's
knees. I like the way the sea smells of spilled milk
on dewy mornings before the southerly gets up,
the horse smell ladies give off when they bend
over you. Make you feel strong, those things,
strong enough to stop her crying. That's what

I do when I lie there, waiting for her to stop. She says there's nothing I can't do if I put my mind to it. So I think of those things. To make me strong. And it's hard work. I'm tired in the mornings.

As the BOY *speaks, the light slowly fades to black, so that his last words are uttered in darkness.*

But when you sleep the world keeps working, moving, like a boat. After you push, it keeps moving. Just a little bit, just a little while. Going somewhere. Taking you, while you sleep. And when you wake up you're ready to push again.

Darkness. Gurglings of water. Things knocking against timbers. Slowly, first light illuminates the high distance. An initial flutter of birdsong. Somewhere a diesel engine arcs up faintly. In the dimness it's possible to make out a mast. But no hull. Splashes, a gasp.

BAXTER: [*unseen*] Fuck! No, no, no, no! She's opened the seacocks!

COL: [*unseen*] What? Whassat?

JACKIE: [*unseen*] Oh, God. Baxter!

Daylight on BAXTER *who sits forlorn in the little red dinghy between* Goodness *and* Mercy.

Only the mast of his boat is visible.

> COL: Scuttled, sabotaged, robbed. It's not bloody
> fair, it's not right! Christ, there's an esky.

> JACKIE: Shut up, Col, and throw him a line.

> BAXTER: No, no. Don't bother.

> JACKIE: What're you talking about?

> BAXTER: Homeless.

> JACKIE: You're insured, aren't you?

He shoots her a knowing look, takes in pieces of his fixed life as they separate around him.

> COL: Son, mate.

BAXTER *takes off his shirt, examines it, holds it to his face a moment and then catches some sense of movement about him. He spreads the shirt above his head as if to catch some wind. On the jetty behind him, the* BOY *holds the dinghy line. He begins to draw* BAXTER *away.*

> JACKIE: What're you doing?

> BAXTER: Don't know.

JACKIE: You alright?

BAXTER: No. Yes. I really don't know. God. I'm
scared.

JACKIE: Grab the line.

BAXTER: No.

COL: Son, your boat, your stuff.

JACKIE: Baxter, grab the line.

BAXTER: Can't. No, I won't.

COL: You've lost everythin, son. Least keep ya wits.

BAXTER: But I'm alright. Really. I think I am.

JACKIE: Where are you going?

BAXTER: I really don't know. Hey, is that a breeze?

COL: There's always a breeze.

BAXTER: Right, yeah. Good, good.

JACKIE: Baxter?

BAXTER: Yes – there, really, I can feel it.

The bird shadow passes over him. He manages a faltering smile.
Blackout.

THE END

The Boy (Kai Arbuckle)

Production Notes

Rising Water was first produced by Black Swan State Theatre Company in Perth, Western Australia, on 25 June 2011, with the following cast:

CAST AND CREW

COL	Geoff Kelso
BAXTER	John Howard
JACKIE	Alison Whyte
DEE	Claire Lovering
BOY	Kai Arbuckle, Callum Fletcher (Alternating)
RAY THE BOATIE, PASSERBY, REVELLER, DRUNKEN BOOFHEAD, SEAGOING GENTLEMAN	Stuart Halusz
DIRECTOR	Kate Cherry
SET AND COSTUME DESIGNER	Christina Smith
LIGHTING DESIGNER	Matt Scott
SOUND DESIGNER AND COMPOSER	Iain Grandage
MOVEMENT DIRECTOR	Lisa Scott-Murphy
ASSOCIATE DIRECTOR	Stuart Halusz
ASSISTANT SET AND COSTUME DESIGNER	Fiona Bruce

Col (Geoff Kelso)

Director's Note

In 2009 I received an email from Tim Winton's agent asking if I would have time to read his first theatre script. Would I ever! I read *Rising Water* that night. Despite Tim's humble trepidation about writing a play, his understanding of theatre and its possibilities shone through even in the first draft of his debut play.

Tim is a masterful storyteller, and his first foray into theatre is no exception. *Rising Water* springs to life through Tim's exquisitely drawn characters, joyous use of the Australian vernacular, sumptuous rendering of a powerful landscape that bursts off the page and his mischievous illumination of a small community. The play demands the large canvas of a theatre space, the humour of actors to give the characters voice and the imagination of a designer to create a space that would contain both the reality of a marina and the promise of magic. Most of all it demands the possibilities of silence that only theatre can provide.

Tim captures the Australian vernacular with his own kind of poetry and dynamism. He creates mythology through his illumination of detail. Tim's characterisations and landscape mean that the play sits in a realism that is familiar to any Australian who lives on the coast. The visitation of two figures, one mysterious and the other prosaic, gently lifts the play out of naturalism into the realm of the magical. Tim's play is rich in satisfying dichotomies: the sacred and the profane, nihilism and hope, poignancy and irreverent humour; and these dichotomies take *Rising Water* into a territory of magic realism that is uniquely Australian.

Rising Water is a play about redemption; hope found in the strangest of places. A foul-mouthed, acid-tongued cynic upends the lives of three middle-aged people clinging to their rituals and their hard-won privacy. The girl's reckless neediness and abandonment have unintended consequences that are at once horrifying and redemptive.

Three boats are docked off a Fremantle marina – one of the few places left in Australia where the rich and poor live side by side, where the skilled sailor may have docked his boat next to one being used as nothing more than a 'floating caravan'. The marina takes centre stage. The boats are islands of isolation and solace for their inhabitants: boat dwellers who have lost the desire to sail, people who prefer to talk about journeys rather than take them.

Rising Water provides a rare insight into one of the few remaining places in Australia where people from different demographics and economic strata live so close to each other that they can hear each other 'take a leak'. It's the perfect situation for a microscopic view of the tenuous social fabric of Western Australia, the boom-bust state.

Tim portrays three unlikely boat dwellers – Col, Baxter and Jackie – with a healthy dose of compassion, poignancy and humour. These characters are each in a limbo of their own making, caught between the promise of land and the mysterious lure of sea. Everything changes on Australia Day, when propelled by the arrival of a mysterious boy and an angry young British tourist, Baxter and Jackie face their demons.

The boats are uniquely reflective of each owner's particular character. Jackie's boat is beautifully cared for and seaworthy, Col's boat has a broken mast that he has not bothered to fix for months and Baxter's is an unlovely and unloved tub, a refuge for a man who gathers the junk of the marina for recreation. Jackie, Col and Baxter have lost the desire to sail, they stare out over the horizon dreaming of daring journeys and foreign lands but each has long ago lost their appetite for adventure.

Ironically, the three live-aboards have come to the marina for anonymity and refuge; instead they are forced to defend their privacy. In a world that places a premium on gathering information, they find themselves embroiled in gossip, innuendo and politics, seeking and repelling intimacy and confidences like magnets. The romance of the marina is quickly domesticated to power plays, broken promises and shattered dreams – just like any other village.

The docked boats are refuges and prisons, islands of lost hopes and faded dreams. Their owners spend most of their time filling the day with noise, witty banter, tall tales and stories that allow them to maintain their closely guarded identities. It is their silences that give Baxter and Jackie their heartbreaking poignancy, their sheer inability to articulate their rich and tormented inner lives. Only in their solo interactions with the audience are the characters truly able to articulate their longings and their losses. They may crave intimacy as much as they shun it, but it takes almost an entire play before Baxter and Jackie are able to hold a gut-wrenchingly honest conversation with each other and truly reveal their private agonies and secret dreams.

The jetty has its own set of rules. On Winton's dock, no-one goes unscathed. Corruption is there for the picking, but even though these boat dwellers are packed tightly together, they survive by choosing deafness and blindness; intimacy is hard fought for, and rarely won.

After reading *Rising Water*, I immediately gave it to Christina Smith, set and costume designer. Her faith in the play, and her imaginative response to it had a major impact on the shaping of its first production. We chose to set the production in a heightened reality, with boats that aren't quite real, and a skyline that reminds us how similar a skyline of masts and a cityscape can be. Three boat owners, a tourist, a series of representational characters and a mysterious boy all inhabit this landscape. Although it's a kind of limbo, this world is never still; the boats are constantly shifting, as are alliances. Christina's inspired set revealed the wisdom and magic of the play, as it illuminated Tim's tale of heartbreak, hope and mystery on the Western Australian seafront.

I am grateful to: Tim Winton for trusting Black Swan State Theatre Company with his first play; Christina Smith for designing a brilliant set that illuminated the play's magic, while celebrating its realism; Matt Scott for his exquisite lighting; Iain Grandage for his unique understanding of the aural world Tim's imagination evokes; and the actors – Geoff Kelso, Claire Lovering, Alison Whyte, John Howard, Stuart Halusz, Kai Arbuckle and Callum Fletcher – for bringing the play to life.

Kate Cherry
Director

Baxter (John Howard)

Signs of Life

Contents

From left: Bender (Tom E. Lewis), Mona (Pauline Whyman),
Georgie (Helen Morse), Lu (George Shevtsov)

SETTING

An isolated farmhouse in a parched olive grove beside a dead and empty river in the not-so-distant future, when drought seems to have become permanent, even apocalyptic.

A tree, the yard, the veranda. A red kite pinned to the wall.

CHARACTERS

GEORGIE	An Australian woman in late middle age, an orchardist recently widowed
BENDER	An Aboriginal man in his thirties, a shooter and itinerant labourer
MONA	Bender's sister, an Aboriginal woman in her forties, an invalid pensioner
LU	Georgie's dead husband, a former fisherman and horticulturalist

SCENE I

Darkness. The sound of crickets. In the gloom, an unlit farmhouse becomes dimly visible. An owl hoots abjectly. Barely perceptible, GEORGIE appears on the veranda. She wears a man's cotton robe, boxer shorts and a singlet. There's an unlit torch in her hand. She peers out into the darkness, listening keenly, as if to the owl itself.

> GEORGIE: You used to say how funny it was – the idea of it. Me. The restless traveller. Coming to live out here. In the middle of nowhere. Amongst the olive trees. With you.

After a few moments the distant noise of a vehicle on a highway; the sound slowly intensifies as it gets closer, until eventually the motor itself is audible. The sound becomes ominous, ever closer. Then the engine falters, sputters and fades to nothing. Crickets reclaim the night for a long moment and then a starter motor begins to natter – once, twice, three times. Sound of a car door creaking open and a bird taking flight from the tree. The sound of the car hood being slammed shut, and then a man's bellow of rage.

BENDER: [*off*] Shit!

MONA: [*off*] Go orn!

BENDER: Shut up.

MONA: I'll do it if you don't!

GEORGIE *takes up a piece of a tree limb from where it stands by the veranda rail.*

BENDER: [*off*] No bloody way! You stay in the car.

GEORGIE *holds the stick at her side, a weapon. A woman (*MONA*) begins to sob and keen faintly out there in the dark. GEORGIE hefts the stick with a little more conviction, her apprehension increasing with every passing moment.*

BENDER: [*off*] Fuck!

GEORGIE: There's a shotgun in the laundry. Box of shells in the linen press. But you said it yourself: step out with a firearm and feel a bad scene get worse in a hurry. *A car door slams and she flinches.*

Sounds so sensible. When your heart's not
thumping like a dog in a box.

The sound of breaking glass.

BENDER: [*off*] Yeah, that's right; that'll help. Ya
stupid bitch.

GEORGIE: C'mon, people, start it up. Keep going,
just go.

MONA: [*off, screaming*] Please!

BENDER: Lemme alone.

MONA: Please, please!

*Footfalls approach. Closer. And then an ominous silence. Until
only crickets are audible. Terrified, GEORGIE turns, as if she's
decided to get the shotgun after all, but before she breaks away:*

BENDER: [*obscured, very close*] Hullo?

*GEORGIE gasps, snaps on the torch and BENDER is caught in
the beam. He looks rough, as if he's been sleeping out.*

GEORGIE: Jesus.

BENDER: Nah, different fulla.

GEORGIE: Car trouble?

BENDER: Amongst other things. Couldn't lend us
a can of petrol, I spose?

GEORGIE: Everything runs on diesel here.

BENDER: Everythin?

GEORGIE: 'Cept the house. That's wind and solar.

BENDER: Don't spose you got a windpower
lawnmower? Solar chainsaw? No petrol at all?

GEORGIE *weighs this up as* BENDER *suffers in the torchlight.*

GEORGIE: Where's your vehicle?

BENDER: Just out past your gate.

GEORGIE: How many people?

BENDER: Two.

GEORGIE: I heard crying.

BENDER: Me sister.

GEORGIE: Where you from?

BENDER: Hard to say.

GEORGIE: Where have you driven from? Today.

BENDER: Today? Just the bridge up there, coupla mile. Yesterdy, Wubin, New Norcia, Mogumber.

GEORGIE: And where're you headed?

BENDER: Yeah, well there's a question.

GEORGIE: Seemed simple enough.

BENDER: Family business. Never simple.

GEORGIE: True.

BENDER *steps tentatively into the light spilling from the house and is humanized a little.* GEORGIE *switches off the torch.*

BENDER: Didn't mean to scare ya.

GEORGIE: Oh, I'm not scared.

BENDER: [*noting the club*] See you're armed.

GEORGIE: You don't know the half of it.

BENDER: How bout I come back in the mornin?

GEORGIE: Back?

BENDER: When it's . . . in the mornin.

GEORGIE: But you said you needed petrol.

BENDER: True.

GEORGIE: So you'll, what, sleep in the car?

BENDER: Wouldn't be the first time.

GEORGIE: With your sister?

BENDER: We're not perverts.

Sound of a car door creaking open.

GEORGIE: What kind of car?

BENDER: Holden. Wouldn't see me in a Ford.

MONA: [*off, but closer, and still distressed*] Bender!

GEORGIE: What's happening? What's she doing? Why's she crying? What've you done to her?

BENDER: [*turning to leave*] Jesus. I'll come back tomorrow.

MONA: [*off*] Boy? Boy?

A gust of wind comes out of the dark.

SCENE 2

The veranda the next day. BENDER *and* MONA *sit at the table, silent and expressionless. Behind them, a red kite is pinned to the wall. After a long silence,* GEORGIE *enters with a tray containing sugar, milk and mugs. She sets it down.* MONA *reaches for the sugar, adds one, two, three spoonfuls to her mug. And then* BENDER *takes four – hesitates – and makes it five. Another awkward silence.*

BENDER: [*tilts his head toward the interior of house*] Lot of books in there.

GEORGIE: Yes.

BENDER: You a teacher, then?

GEORGIE: No. They're my husband's.

BENDER: He's a teacher, then?

GEORGIE: No.

BENDER: It's just a lotta books. If ya not a teacher.

Pause.

BENDER: This your husband's place, then?

GEORGIE: Yes.

Pause.

GEORGIE: Your car.

BENDER: HT. With the 186.

GEORGIE: We'll get it going in a minute.
[*an awkward pause*] By the look of it you've been
travelling a while. [*only silence*] Lot of red dust.
[*another long, fruitless pause*] You Noongar people
or Yamatji?

BENDER: That car's been all over.

GEORGIE: I saw the red dirt. Wondered if you were
from up north, like, like Martu people, but—

BENDER: Not dark enough? That what you thinkin?

GEORGIE: No! It's just the plates on the car. Meekatharra—

BENDER: They was on it when I bought it.

GEORGIE: So . . . you're from there?

BENDER: Nup. Not really. What are you, anyway, some kinda Aborigine spotter?

GEORGIE: Pardon?

BENDER: Bit of an expert?

GEORGIE: No.

BENDER: Like some people with birds and stuff. Lookin for special markins.

GEORGIE: I'm sorry, I—

BENDER: I'm a tired, dusty, fed-up blackfulla, that's what kind I am.

GEORGIE: I didn't mean . . . It's just . . . well, I haven't seen anyone for a while. I'm out of practice.

A long, uncomfortable pause ensues.

BENDER: That river come up onto this place?

GEORGIE *instinctively looks out toward the dead river.*

> GEORGIE: Well, used to. Ran the whole length of
> the property.

> MONA: Property. Properly. Property.

> BENDER: Moore River.

> GEORGIE: Poor, dead thing. Makes a big bend as it
> passes. Well, did until a few years ago. Now it's just
> dry sand, mostly. But you can see where it was. Like
> the outline of a dinosaur. A skeleton. I go out some
> evenings and look at it, try to imagine it alive again.

> MONA: This the one, Bub. This the place.

BENDER *is affected by what his sister has said.* MONA *gets up
and stares out into the distance. She feels something, a presence.*

> BENDER: [*looking at the kite*] You got kids?

> GEORGIE: I was a wicked stepmother once.

> BENDER: What?

> GEORGIE: But, no, no children of my own. You?

BENDER's *not really listening; he's trying to figure out why
there's a kite on this woman's wall.*

BENDER: Hm?

GEORGIE: Do you have children?

He shakes his head.

BENDER: Was an uncle once.

GEORGIE: Oh?

BENDER: Felt good.

LU *appears, watching on with interest from within the olive tree.* MONA *begins to weep.*

GEORGIE: Something wrong? Is she alright?

BENDER: Right as she'll ever be.

GEORGIE *begins to go to* MONA.

BENDER: Leave it. Please.

MONA *continues to weep as the light fades and wattlebirds and cockatoos overtake the night and a gust of wind rolls through. Suddenly* MONA *is startled, galvanized by something unseen, something that seems to have passed by.*

MONA: Boy? Bobby?

BENDER: [*irritated*] What are ya doin?

MONA: [*confused, then sly*] Somethin. Nothin.

MONA *peers out anxiously, longingly.*

GEORGIE: Nothing out there anymore, nothing alive. Except for a few wild dogs.

BENDER: Dingoes?

GEORGIE: No, just feral dogs. Starving. Not even any roadkill now.

BENDER: They'll turn on each other. In the end.

GEORGIE: Like humans, no doubt.

BENDER: And when the last one's left it'll eat its own shit, 'fore it dies.

GEORGIE: How do you know?

BENDER: Seen it plenty times. Happens more'n more now.

GEORGIE: Whole country's—

BENDER: Dyin.

GEORGIE: Wasting away, like . . . a body
consuming itself, fat, muscle . . . tendon.

BENDER: Just hangin on.

GEORGIE: Barely. Only a few birds now.

BENDER: No rain, nothin breedin.

GEORGIE: Even the aquifers are drying up. See the
stress in the trees, like they're growing old before
your eyes.

BENDER: Still, must be somethin here, keep a few
dogs goin.

GEORGIE: There's a bore. The windmill. But it's
gasping.

BENDER: Suckin the dregs.

GEORGIE: The dogs come around after dark,
when it's safe. Drink from the old cattle trough.
I should fence it off, cover it. But then I think
about the honeyeaters and wattlebirds, the
cockies and the peewees.

BENDER: Need to shoot 'em.

GEORGIE: The birds?

BENDER: Nah, them dogs.

GEORGIE: No.

BENDER: Why not?

GEORGIE: I can't.

BENDER: Ya must have a shotty. Saw a box of shells.

GEORGIE: What?

BENDER: Four-ten. Number four shot Bismuth.
    Good ammo.

GEORGIE: And where'd you find that?

BENDER: Cupboard with the sheets. Saw a gittar, too.

MONA *turns their way and mimes drawing a bead on*
BENDER *and shoots.*

MONA: Shooter.

GEORGIE: [*disturbed*] Sorry?

MONA: He's a shooter.

GEORGIE: Oh. Like, a roo shooter?

BENDER: Well, more of a dogger.

MONA *lets off an unnerving cat-like yowl.*

BENDER: Stop it!

MONA *gets up and walks away from them, stands alone, tormented by something in her head, like a swarm of bees.*

BENDER: Last job I did was all cats. Wildlife mob. Up the peninsula. Special program. They're breedin woylies and boodies and little rare wallaby, you know, lost fullas?

GEORGIE: Extinct?

BENDER: Thass right. They got this big electric fence.

GEORGIE: Lucky them.

BENDER: Keeps out foxes and cats. Foxes you can bait from the air.

GEORGIE: Ten-eighty.

BENDER: But bloody cats, you gotta trap the buggers. Kill everythin, cats. Lizards, birds, turtle, everythin.

GEORGIE: So, what . . . you're clearing out feral cats inside the—

BENDER: Sanctuary.

GEORGIE: So the marsupials can breed?

BENDER: Correct. Like an island.

GEORGIE: Sanctuary.

BENDER: Good job, decent pay. Make their own drinkin water from the sea. Nice people, science fullas; well, nice enough. But a good feelin, ya know? Takin rubbish out, puttin proper animals back. Like bringin back life to country. You know what I mean?

GEORGIE: Yes. I think so. But if it doesn't rain again—

BENDER: Then we all buggered. It's over.

GEORGIE: Hard to imagine. Everything finished, actually over.

BENDER: Don't even bloody wanna think about it.

GEORGIE: Isn't there a bird, some sacred bird that heralds the coming of the rain?

BENDER: Where'd you read that, in ya big
    Aborigine book?

GEORGIE: Well, isn't there?

BENDER: No idea. But you can lend me the book
    and I'll study up. I can stand on one leg, if it
    helps.

GEORGIE *regards him a moment, as if seeing him differently.*
MONA *sits absently, abjectly completely alone at so short a*
distance.

GEORGIE: You like it. Bringing life back to
    country.

BENDER: True.

GEORGIE: Seems a strange way to bring life,
    though, doesn't it? Trapping, shooting, killing.

BENDER: Well. It's not pretty.

GEORGIE: I couldn't do it.

BENDER: Good. I could do without the
    competition.

GEORGIE: I suppose I'm too soft.

BENDER: Or just sentimental.

GEORGIE: There's a difference?

BENDER: Soft is when you let yourself feel. That's good. You need that. Sentimental, but? That's when ya only let yourself feel, and you stop thinkin. That's when people're dangerous.

GEORGIE: And it doesn't bother you, all the killing?

BENDER: Killed things all me life. To eat. For money. Old man, he told me, orright to feel sad. Even a bream, you pull him from a creek and then you think, Poor thing, and then you eat him. Cats, but? Killin them murderin bastards? Never felt a thing.

GEORGIE: So, the job—

BENDER: Had to leave early. Family business.

MONA *is suddenly alert.*

MONA: Bobby!

MONA *exits, searching.*

BENDER: Mona, git here! Break ya bloody leg out there. King browns everywhere.

GEORGIE: I haven't seen a snake for a year.

MONA: Bobby?

BENDER: Don't make me come out there'n git ya! Bloody sick of it. [*angry, menacing*] You heard me. Mona!

MONA *shuffles back, steps up onto the veranda, seems a little disoriented, then fixes on* BENDER, *pointing slyly at him, drilling into him in a way that unnerves him.*

MONA: Kill anythin, my little brother. Anythin what moves. But he can't make somethin come alive. Not one thing!

In the fraught silence that ensues, MONA *goes inside.* BENDER *collects the tea tray. A door slams indoors.*

BENDER: Listen. Thanks for the petrol – and everythin.

GEORGIE: You're welcome.

BENDER: But that carbie's not right.

GEORGIE: Let's have a look at it.

BENDER: Bit hard now, in the dark. And Mona, she's—

GEORGIE: I'm sure she's as keen to get on the road as you are.

BENDER: Keen, orright, that's her. [*bitterly*] Keen as bloody mustard.

GEORGIE: So—

Something crashes inside the house.

MONA: Bastard!

BENDER: So we'll get it right in the mornin.

BENDER *goes indoors.* GEORGIE *sits in bewilderment.*

BENDER: [*off*] Christ, you're a waste of skin!

MONA: [*off*] Get fucked, you.

BENDER: Fuckin sick of ya.

GEORGIE *steps away in increasing apprehension. From within the tree* LU *watches.*

GEORGIE: I can't do this. I've taken them in, fed them, given precious fuel, done everything

decent, but all I want is for him to take the parcel
of food I've made up, put that poor, wretched
woman into his clapped-out station wagon and
bump on down the drive. Is that so terrible? It's
too much, too sudden – visitors, conversation,
strangers – and I've got my own decisions to
make. You know that, you understand that,
don't you? I should have gone by now. Nothing
to stay for. But I'm tired. Dry as a leaf. I just
want to be in bed, sink into the pillow that still
smells of you, look at your boots there, licked by
moonlight. Sleep. And dream it's all okay, that
everything is still what it was.

Inside the house MONA *and* BENDER *shuffle about opening
cupboards and doors, trying to get a station on the radio,
skidding back chairs, murmuring, bitching.*

BENDER: [*off*] What're you lookin at me like that for?

MONA: [*off*] Weak, you.

BENDER: Bugger off.

MONA: Weak.

BENDER: Shut up or I swear, woman, I'll take you
straight back.

MONA: Woulden dare!

BENDER: Just try me.

GEORGIE: I'm safe, Lu. Aren't I?

MONA: [*off*] Here. This the place. This the story.

BENDER: [*off*] Just shut up. Please.

MONA: Kept you under a blanket, kept you safe.

BENDER: Go to sleep.

MONA: [*beginning to weep*] All them times she's wild and crazy. Keep you safe, little brother.

BENDER: Mona, fuck!

MONA: And you talk about sendin me back? That madhouse? Now we here, in the story, you fuckin talk about putting me back?

BENDER: Git off me, piss off!

MONA: You evil!

Sounds of a scuffle, a chair skids, someone thumps into the wall. GEORGIE *takes up the stick, afraid.*

GEORGIE: They'll be gone in the morning. Won't they?

MONA *screams cries and wails, winding down into sad hoots of grief until there's only fraught silence. And then, finally, as if venturing into the yawning gap, the sound of an owl.*
Three mournful hoots.

> GEORGIE: There it is again. Invisible. In some
> dying tree. Out there in a bare, dry paddock
> under moonlight where nothing moves.
> Watching. Just a solitary ghost-eyed bird,
> waiting for a twitch, a flicker, any sign of life,
> for company as much as food. Desolate, lonely.
> That's what it'll sound like, the last bird on earth,
> staring, peering into the endless, empty night,
> calling out to nothing at all.

The sound of beating wings.

SCENE 3

Cockatoos screech and chatter above the veranda in the afternoon. At the table MONA *stares into space.* BENDER *has an old newspaper on the table and some small tools. He tinkers with his carburettor and a screwdriver.* GEORGIE *steps out, squinting in the light. She surveys her guests, hesitates, cocks her head, listening.*

GEORGIE: The fridge. It's stopped.

BENDER: Fixed.

GEORGIE: Fixed?

BENDER: Bloody thing runs day'n night. Man can hardly sleep.

MONA: What, snore when you're awake, now?

BENDER: Thermostat.

MONA: Makes him snore all night when he can't hardly sleep.

GEORGIE: I should have . . . it's like I'm still waiting for him to fix it.

BENDER: [*taking this in*] Refrigeration. Whitefulla magic, eh?

MONA: [*ruefully*] Cold beer, true.

The siblings glare at one another in a manner GEORGIE *cannot read.*

GEORGIE: Sure you don't want me to look at that carburettor?

BENDER: I got it.

GEORGIE: After five hours?

BENDER: Book in there. Next to the piano.

GEORGIE: Yes?

BENDER: *The Secret.*

GEORGIE: Oh. God.

BENDER: What's that about?

GEORGIE: I dunno; I couldn't finish it. Some kind of self-help book.

BENDER: Help yourself do what?

GEORGIE: Make money, as far as I can see.

BENDER: Money.

GEORGIE: My sister gave it to me.

BENDER: She rich, then?

GEORGIE: Well, as it happens.

BENDER: What she do, what's her secret?

GEORGIE: She marries.

BENDER: Ah. That secret.

MONA: [*urging* BENDER] Family business.

GEORGIE: Spoilt white woman business.

BENDER *smiles.*

MONA: [*to* BENDER] Ask her.

MONA's *interjection breaks the light mood.* BENDER *is both irritated and discomfited.*

MONA: Go orn.

BENDER: All them olive trees. What's the point?

GEORGIE: Oil, mostly.

MONA: Not what I'm talkin about, Bub.

BENDER: Olives. Never liked 'em. Like eatin salt, like . . . like blood. And straight off the tree? Jesus, I thought I'd die. Tasted it for a week. Like battery acid and dogshit.

MONA: Useless bugger.

BENDER: Shut up.

MONA: Missus?

GEORGIE: Georgie. Call me Georgie.

MONA: A man live here before? Man up a pole? Sittin up this pole. High up.

BENDER: Seventy year ago, maybe.

MONA: Out in a paddock, all day up a pole.

GEORGIE: A pole? Oh. Yes. Good grief. Wally Fox, Lu's father, my husband's father. I know about that; I mean, I've heard about it. It was a bit of a fad for a while. People did it for a lark, on a dare, to raise money. But old Wally, he was different, apparently. Bit of an eccentric.

BENDER: Eccentric! Polite way of callin a bloke a fuckin weirdo.

MONA: [*to* BENDER] Show respeck!

BENDER: Climb down off ya broomstick for five minutes, willya?

MONA: [*to* BENDER] The river!

Pause.

MONA: Bub, the river!

GEORGIE: I'm sorry, I don't follow.

GEORGIE *gets nothing from* MONA *whose focus is intensely on* BENDER.

GEORGIE: Pole-sitting, the river. What are we talking about here?

BENDER: Well. I was gunna ask. If you wouldn't

mind. [MONA *looms, urges, threatens at every hesitation*] If we could maybe . . . me'n Mona . . . if we could go down the river a minute. For a look-see?

GEORGIE: Well, as I said, there's almost no water anymore. A couple of rancid puddles and a dead billabong just downstream—

MONA: Don't care. Doesn't matter.

BENDER: Mona, just—

MONA: For a look.

GEORGIE: Of course. [*unable to refrain from irony*] Be my guest.

But MONA *and* BENDER *don't move.* GEORGIE *is bewildered.*

GEORGIE: The track's right there past the shed. You just follow the tree line down . . . it's right . . .

GEORGIE *is up, ready to show them, but neither* MONA *nor* BENDER *has made a move.*

BENDER: Better in the morning.

GEORGIE: The morning? But . . .

BENDER: Can't do it today.

MONA: Plenty shadows.

BENDER: Yeah, more light. Need more light.

GEORGIE: But it'll be the same tomorrow.

BENDER: Still. I'll be better then.

GEORGIE: You're not well?

BENDER: I'm . . .

MONA: You not strong, that's what. No balls.

BENDER: Well, Sistergirl, you bloody go!

MONA: Together. You said together. You promised!

BENDER: Tomorrow, I said. You heard the lady.

GEORGIE: Georgie.

BENDER: Tomorrow.

GEORGIE: Tomorrow?

BENDER: Time to think.

GEORGIE: Oh. To think.

MONA: Get strong.

BENDER: If you don't mind.

GEORGIE: [*dejected*] Oh. Why would I mind?

BENDER: [*exiting*] Fix this bloody thing.

MONA *goes inside. A gust of wind, voices, steel guitar, until:*

SCENE 4

The veranda the same evening. GEORGIE *stands alone on the step with a mug of tea. She walks out to the house tree. As* GEORGIE *speaks,* LU *appears in the tree.*

GEORGIE: A man up a pole in a paddock. Sound familiar? That sort of caper ran in the family, didn't it? You people. Stiffnecked, wayward, weirdos. If everyone else in the world decided to walk east you'd go west. Just to be different.

LU: [*climbing down beside her*] Oh, I dunno about that.

GEORGIE: You could be standing in a downpour and say it wasn't raining.

LU: Bollocks.

GEORGIE: First day I saw you.

LU: I think it was night-time, actually.

GEORGIE: Thinking to myself, Hullo, this is different.

LU: Eccentric.

GEORGIE: Creeping around like a thief, you were.

LU: Off the grid, that's all.

GEORGIE: Paperwork-averse.

LU: Fish, crays, abalone. Cash in hand. Tax-free.

GEORGIE: Unlicensed.

LU: Aspirational.

GEORGIE: Poaching up and down the coast under cover of darkness.

LU: Saves getting sunburnt.

GEORGIE: Nuts, all of you.

LU: Mixed nuts.

GEORGIE: Salty nuts. Like father, like son.

LU: No, not him. Think I was more like my mother. She loved the world. All that lives is holy, she said. Beautiful.

GEORGIE: Beautiful man. Fell for you like a brittle tree in a gust of wind. One sweet puff. As if I'd been standing there all my life, just waiting to fall, waiting for that breeze, that weird angle, to bowl me over, root and branch. What a lovely catastrophe.

LU: Awkward. But yes, it was lovely.

GEORGIE: Then to come here to this empty house in the bare paddocks.

LU: Not empty. There was a piano, books.

GEORGIE: True.

LU: And music. Always music. Veranda music, dirt music.

GEORGIE: Bare earth down to the river.

LU: Melon vines. Like green lace.

GEORGIE: The actual running river.

LU: Watermelon, rockies, honeydew, grew 'em all.

GEORGIE: Solar panels, wind turbine. And no satellite dish.

LU: Weirdo.

GEORGIE: Hardly an olive tree on the place then.

LU: The old man was a hard-arse. He said this world is just a passing dream – shit and gristle. Only had his eye on Heaven. Far as he was concerned matter didn't matter a bit. But Mum still planted trees. Planted that one there, the very first. She loved the world. He was nay and she was yea.

GEORGIE: I wish I'd known her. Back then, when we were so much younger.

LU: And the world still alive.

GEORGIE: Everything standing up alive.

LU: Behold, I see men as trees walking!

GEORGIE: They said you were a weirdo.

LU: Your weirdo.

GEORGIE: But you always went too far.

LU: For you.

GEORGIE: Oh, bullshit. It's in your nature.

LU: You think?

GEORGIE: Always going too deep, too far from ordinary. And when you were like that, so wilful and reckless, I felt abandoned.

LU: Some places you go to alone. Have to.

GEORGIE: I used to steel myself for bad news, like an army bride, always scared you'd push things too far. Not just the rednecks, the cops, the Fisheries, but what your body could tolerate—

LU: Four minutes, that's how long I could hold my breath.

GEORGIE: Just to poach a few crays.

LU: They seek him here, they seek him there, they seek him in his underwear. Man had to make a living.

GEORGIE: Come on, it was an addiction. You did it for the thrill, to get away with it.

LU: Right under their noses, all those White Point big-shots.

GEORGIE: And didn't that run in the family.

LU: But when it got too hard, when I got old, what I really missed was the sea.

GEORGIE: I know.

LU: The single breath, the feel of the water, the privacy of that long glide down in the quiet, with only the drumbeat of blood in my ears.

GEORGIE: You make it sound so bloody romantic—

LU: Well—

GEORGIE: But you don't know what it looks like when it all goes wrong. You've never pulled someone from the water all sleepy and smiley and blue in the face like a poisoned junkie.

LU: Geez, it was only the once.

GEORGIE: Why should a person have to see that on the face of someone they love?

LU: Slapping me back to life.

GEORGIE: Instinct, I suppose, and all those years of nursing.

LU: Like an angry angel.

GEORGIE: I was afraid, panicked.

LU: You were terrific. That day and every day that followed.

GEORGIE: I didn't think it'd work.

LU: The CPR?

GEORGIE: Us. Me. Here. Maybe we should have gone somewhere different, fresh.

LU: I couldn't. This is where all the stories are, the songs—

GEORGIE: Ghosts.

LU: Family, love.

GEORGIE: Went numb, I think. Once it stopped raining. Stopped paying attention, that's the thing. Because I should have seen it coming. Once you started having those dreams.

LU: Everyone dreams of flying.

GEORGIE: That wasn't flying, it was falling.

LU: Not nightmares. I wasn't afraid.

GEORGIE: Maybe you should have been.

LU: It wasn't like falling from grace, just falling to earth. Hurtling at the dirt: dry leaves, beetles, dead grass rushing up, suddenly—

GEORGIE: Huge—

LU: Planetary—

GEORGIE: Geological.

LU: Made you laugh, didn't it?

BENDER *comes out onto the veranda.*

BENDER: Someone out there?

GEORGIE: What? No.

An owl hoots.

BENDER: Can't find Mona.

MONA: [*off*] Nooo! Please!

SCENE 5

MONA *lurches drunkenly in from the yard, chasing a phantom, a vodka bottle in one hand, distressed, hopeful, cajoling.*

BENDER: Mona?

MONA: Bobby? Carn Bobby love. C'mere, give ya ole mum a kiss, eh? Doan ya wanna. Carn, doan run away. Bobby?

BENDER: What the fuck?

MONA: Didden mean it! Sorry baby!

BENDER: Mona, gimme that, now, give it here. Just give me the fuckin bottle.

GEORGIE: What's she doing? She's been in the tractor shed.

BENDER: Can't give her grog.

GEORGIE: I didn't give her anything.

MONA: Doan listen to him.

BENDER: Christ, you didn't tell me you had grog.

GEORGIE: You didn't ask me.

BENDER: What is it?

GEORGIE: Vodka.

BENDER: Fuckin vodka.

GEORGIE: Made in China.

MONA: Done the job.

BENDER *seizes the bottle.*

BENDER: Come here, come on.

MONA: Fuggin bastards.

GEORGIE: Here.

MONA: Found ya secret spot.

BENDER: Yeah, well that worked out real good,
    didn't it, Sis?

MONA: Takes one to know one, eh? I know all the
    secret spots.

GEORGIE: So it would seem.

BENDER: Careful, she's . . . Oh, Jesus.

GEORGIE: It's perfectly alright.

MONA: Perfegly.

GEORGIE: I'm a nurse.

MONA *turns and spits in* GEORGIE*'s face.* GEORGIE *recoils.*

GEORGIE: Well, used to be.

BENDER: She doesn't know what she's doin.

GEORGIE: Well, there's a luxury.

BENDER: Go on, I'll fix it.

GEORGIE: It's fine. I'll give you a hand. I can deal
    with this.

BENDER: No. It's family business.

MONA: What fuggin family?

BENDER: Please. Just gimme a minute.

BENDER *hands the bottle to* GEORGIE *who takes it reluctantly and retreats to watch from the doorway.*

BENDER: Jesus, Mona.

MONA: Get fucked, you.

BENDER: Quit a good job for ya.

MONA: You not the bossa me!

BENDER: Best job in me fuckin life. Drive down two days and nights to get you outta that place and fer what?

MONA: Told you fer what.

BENDER: So I can drive around the country for a week, sleepin in the car, livin like some—

MONA: Blackfulla.

BENDER: Jesus, Mona, ya couldn't keep it together this long.

MONA: Ya promised.

BENDER: Eight fuckin days, that's all ya last.

MONA: Ninety-seven days sober!

BENDER: Ya better off back in there. Where ya can't get any.

MONA: Just kill me. I'm nothin.

BENDER: Shut up.

MONA: Bender, just kill me!

BENDER: I said shut up.

She lunges at him, tries to scratch his face and he slaps her, and she falls to the dirt where he hugs her in remorse. She beats her own head, weeping. And stops suddenly, in a moment of clarity.

MONA: Please, little brother. Here.

BENDER: It's just somewhere else on the road, Sis.

MONA: Here's good. Here's right. I can feel him.

BENDER: What're you talking about?

MONA: He was here. I can feel him close-up.

BENDER: You're drunk.

MONA: But I can feel him here!

BENDER: The boy?

MONA: No. Not him.

BENDER: What're you talking about?

MONA: Pa. He was here. I can feel him close-up.

BENDER: It's orright, okay. Whatever you reckon.

MONA: This the one, this the place. You remember
the story?

BENDER: Yeah, Sis, I remember.

MONA: Better remember.

BENDER: Jesus, I remember, orright?

MONA: Olive tree. Olive tree.

BENDER: Teacher tied him to an olive tree.

MONA: Tied him with a belt.

BENDER: He's barefoot—

MONA: Pa—

BENDER: Short pants, big-eyed, done something wrong, forgot his four times tables, his God Save the Queen. And he's . . .

MONA: Howlin.

BENDER: Teacher cuts a switch with his pocket knife. Just reached up, took a branch, stripped the fruit, the leaves. Everyone suddenly quiet, all them Mission kids.

MONA: Shh.

BENDER: That teacher, he's a shiny-hair religious man. Half minister, half psychopath.

MONA: Psycho.

BENDER: And kids're watchin, hardly breathin. Sound of them olives fallin on the yellow dirt. Real Bible tree, that olive. Extendin the olive branch. Yep, that's how ya do it. Real Mr Whippy, that stick. Flogged him with it till he pissed himself. Front of thirty other kids, seven, eight—

MONA: Nine year old.

BENDER: For his own good. Where'd he go, that little boy?

MONA: Inside, in deep.

BENDER: Pa.

MONA: He was hard.

BENDER: Like wandoo.

MONA: Ironwood.

BENDER: Most the time he said nothin. Get this, pass that, shut up, youse kids or I'll flog youse. Never said nothin!

MONA: Wanted to live a long time. Wanted grandkids. Shot roos for half a man's wages. Drove that bus from Moora to Marble Bar. Went to a lot of funerals. Died thinkin—

BENDER: Of his mother. In the dialysis ward.

MONA: Alone.

An owl calls.

BENDER: Pa?

BENDER *peers into the dark, a little spooked.*

BENDER: Nuh, it's dogs. I'll get you a blanket.

He gets up to go. GEORGIE *retreats guiltily into the house and* BENDER *follows as the night changes colour.*

SCENE 6

Night-time. On the horizon a reddish glow. MONA *is alone on the veranda step in her t-shirt nightie. She rocks gently. From the glowing tree* LU *emerges to sit beside her.*

> MONA: Not proper. Not right. Never finish. [*she covers her eyes*] Can't put him out. Not proper. Not right. Never finish. Can't put him out. Not proper. Not right. Never finish. Can't, can't, can't, can't, can't put him out.

> LU: Just a bushfire.

> MONA: No. Ahh!

> LU: It'll burn its way to the coast by morning.

> MONA: Bobby.

LU: And tonight, when the breeze dies, it'll be
    raining ash. Soft, powdery. Curling flakes,
    like little boats. Landing in your hair, on your
    tongue. Carbon. Softer than rain. Like him. Like
    me. Stardust.

MONA: Bobby.

LU: Soft as a whisper.

MONA: Gorn.

LU: No. Never.

LU *stands, takes ash from his pockets, spills and sprinkles it
around her, upon her. MONA scoops some onto her head in
sorrow and penitence. She rocks.*

MONA: Sorry, Pa. I'll be good. You was here.
    Weren't you? Weren't you?

The breeze stirs as LU *retreats to the tree. Fire roars and
crackles. MONA winds down, rocking ever slower. BENDER
brings a blanket and lays it out as MONA yawns, fading
fast.*

BENDER: Carn, Sis, let's get you down.

He settles her on the swag and caresses her tenderly.

BENDER: You're orright, Big Sister. I gotcha.

She sleeps, holds his hand to her, like a doll, a child, a memory. And a gust of wind stirs the windmill, the loose sheets of iron on the roof, the haggard ranks of unseen trees.

SCENE 7

Cockatoos shriek in passing and there is bright sunlight upon the veranda next morning. Out on the dirt BENDER inspects a shredded tyre in the yard. Up on the veranda MONA sleeps, curled like a child, and GEORGIE emerges with two mugs of tea. She brings one down for BENDER who pauses in his work to accept it.

GEORGIE: Please tell me that's just the spare.

BENDER: It's rooted.

GEORGIE: Well, it's done some miles by the look of it.

BENDER: Know how that feels.

GEORGIE: Yeah, shredded on the inside, and losing your grip everywhere else.

BENDER: Look, sorry about Mona. She's hard goin when she's sober, but when she's on the charge – Jesus. Like her mother. Alkies, eh?

GEORGIE: [*uncomfortably*] Well, yes.

BENDER: You got a sister.

GEORGIE: Two. One likes the booze. The other's got a thing for benzodiazapines.

BENDER: What's that – drugs?

GEORGIE: Respectable drugs.

BENDER: This the rich one?

GEORGIE: Yep.

BENDER: Money, respectable drugs – gunna read that book.

GEORGIE: Well, look out you don't end up like her.

BENDER: On, what, benzo-diaphrams?

GEORGIE: And a boob job.

BENDER: No way.

GEORGIE: True story.

BENDER: Look out! [*snorts, inclines his head toward the shed*] That boat. In the big shed.

GEORGIE: You mean the shed with the really big lock.

BENDER: Near on twenty foot, that boat.

GEORGIE: Well, you're thorough, I'll give you that.

BENDER: Saw them big ole outboards on it. Hondas.

GEORGIE: Four-stroke. First of the low-emission motors.

BENDER: Petrol motors.

GEORGIE: Heavy as hell, the Hondas, but they're quiet. Just about antiques. And the fuel in the tank's stale, needs draining.

BENDER: You know about boats, then?

GEORGIE: A thing or two.

Pause.

BENDER: *Toota.*

GEORGIE: What?

BENDER: Big ole photo in the boat shed.

GEORGIE: No stone unturned.

BENDER: Fancy frame an everythin.

GEORGIE: Make yourself at home.

BENDER: Photo's there, hangin off a nail, covered in dust. Big white sailboat.

GEORGIE: Yacht.

BENDER: Bloke can't help bein curious.

GEORGIE: Evidently.

BENDER: I'm thinking: Toota, Toota. What kinda name's that?

GEORGIE: *Teuta.*

BENDER: *Teuta?*

GEORGIE: She was a warrior.

BENDER: Like you. Bit of a worrier.

GEORGIE: Warrior.

BENDER: Yer husband's, was it?

GEORGIE: She was mine.

BENDER: Huh.

GEORGIE: Teuta. She was a pirate queen.

BENDER: Bit of fun on the river.

GEORGIE: No, she was a serious boat, an ocean boat.

BENDER: Bugger me. Pirate Princess. To Rottnest Island on a Saturdy arvo.

GEORGIE: Sailed her to Indonesia.

BENDER: No way.

GEORGIE: Just the once. Most of it singlehanded.

BENDER: No bloke?

GEORGIE: Oh, I took one, but he spent half the trip seasick. Rest of the time he was useless anyway.

BENDER: Your husband?

GEORGIE: No, another bloke.

BENDER: Indonesia. That's a long way.

GEORGIE: I'm a good navigator. Always was.

BENDER: Never got lost?

GEORGIE: Not sailing, no.

BENDER: Not once?

GEORGIE: I don't think I knew what it meant to be lost until I was forty.

BENDER: Late developer.

GEORGIE: But I made up for it when I did. Big time. Lost the plot.

BENDER: What're you talkin about?

GEORGIE: Oh. Well, I suppose I kind of fell out of love.

BENDER: What? With the bloke?

GEORGIE: No, with the people I knew, my family, that version of myself. I grew up with a kind of absolute certainty. And somehow it evaporated.

BENDER: Certainty.

GEORGIE: About where I was headed. In my life. I'd always been safe. I belonged. Had all the rituals of the tribe. Leafy riverside suburb, private school, uni, yacht club. All mapped out, you know?

BENDER: No. I don't know.

GEORGIE: I could see it all before me, already organized, my entire life, and I panicked. Bolted. But once I turned my back on it, there were suddenly no landmarks, nothing to steer by but my own judgement. And I really was lost. I wasn't safe.

BENDER: Christ, sounds safe enough to me. Leafy.

GEORGIE: Well, it wasn't leafy. I was in Jeddah at the time.

BENDER: Where's that, Queensland?

GEORGIE: Saudi Arabia.

BENDER: Jesus, you were lost.

GEORGIE: Don't mock me, I was homeless, unemployed, terrified.

BENDER: Ah, bullshit.

GEORGIE: How dare you.

BENDER: You don't know what fear is.

GEORGIE: You've got a bloody nerve.

BENDER: I don't mean feelin anxious. I don't mean little bit insecure. I'm talkin shittin yourself.

GEORGIE: What is this, a competition?

BENDER: If it was, you'd lose it.

GEORGIE: Lucky me. I guess that means I win.

BENDER: [*relenting*] Nil all, draw.

GEORGIE: Says you.

BENDER: Well, you started out interestin enough. Before the sob story. What's all this private school homeless shit got to do with sailin a boat to Indonesia?

GEORGIE: You ever heard of the Zuytdorp Cliffs?

BENDER: Heard of 'em? I been there.

GEORGIE: Two hundred miles long.

BENDER: Like I said, I been there. Shootin goats. Rocky, dry, windblown bloody country. Nearly died of boredom.

GEORGE: Well, I guess you've never seen it from the sea, then.

BENDER: Yeah, funny that, I never could find the keys to me yacht.

GEORGIE: Not so boring from out there.

BENDER: Cliffs is cliffs.

GEORGIE: No, not when you're underneath them, not when you're about to smash into them.

BENDER: Give you a bad moment, did it?

GEORGIE *hesitates.*

GEORGIE: I better check the house batteries.

BENDER: And that's it? That's ya story?

GEORGIE: Well, you're a busy man. I wouldn't want to bore you.

BENDER: So what happened?

GEORGIE: I got caught in a storm.

BENDER: And?

GEORGIE *is reluctant now, demurs.*

BENDER: Come on. Leave a man hangin.

GEORGIE: Well, I'm out there. Singlehanded, more or less. I'm halfway along the cliffs, heading for Shark Bay. The wind's been force five all day, and then it changes direction completely and just builds, you know, until it's a full gale. Waves like buildings. The sea's all streaky spume. And we're getting pounded, hammered, pummelled, flogged.

BENDER: Yeah, yeah, I get it, Jesus. What happened?

GEORGIE: I'm trying to beat clear of the cliffs and the sun goes down and I've got these huge, hissing swells coming at me in the dark from two, three directions all at once, and any moment one could knock you down flat.

BENDER: Can't you pull in somewhere?

GEORGIE: There's nowhere, remember? Not for a hundred miles.

BENDER: Can't you use the motor?

GEORGIE: I've got it going flat out but I'm just motoring on the spot.

BENDER: With the cliffs behind ya.

GEORGIE: I can hear them, see them in the dark. And I can't believe what the mast's doing; it's shivering and shimmying. Oh, God. And then something comes down out of the dark, like a big, roaring road train. Blam. And it's total knockdown, three hundred and sixty degrees. Everything coming to pieces around me. A few seconds later we're upright again. But the mast's gone, the engine's dead and once I've convinced myself that I'm still alive there's nothing to do but cut everything away and lie to. No sail, sea anchor off the bow, dead in the water. At sea that's as close as you get to hiding. Lying to. All night, powerless, expecting to die any minute. Those cliffs closer all the time. Yes, I was scared. I thought I was going to die.

BENDER: Not bad.

GEORGIE: What?

BENDER: Nobody made you go. You chose to
be there.

GEORGIE: What's that got to do with it?

BENDER: You really don't know? You really need
to ask me that?

GEORGIE: Don't tell me – you've got a better story.

BENDER: Well, it's no sailin princess in it, nothing
fancy. Just a life.

GEORGIE: So tell me.

BENDER: Nah, you doan wanna hear it.

GEORGIE: Tell me.

BENDER: Well . . . we was never steerin. Mona'n
me. Went where the wind took us. Ship we sailed
in was a bus.

GEORGIE: A bus?

BENDER: Lived in it, Pa's bus. Ten, fifteen years,
maybe. Good old bus. Leyland Tiger. Front
engine job. Always goin somewhere. New town,

cattle station, different people. But, sometimes.
Well, like you'n them cliffs. Just a big ole storm
come down and it feels like there's no one drivin.
Mum goin crazy, fightin, getting locked up. She
come and went, Mum. Mostly went. And Pa, he
had these moods. Got hollow and dead inside,
like his spirit was extinct. Then he was a stranger.
And when he was like that – Christ – I got scared.
Pissed me pants sometimes. It was like he might
do anythin, say anythin. We didn't know him.
Me'n Mona, we'd hide down under the seats till
it was all over, that horrible . . . stormin, wordless
rage. What you call that? With no sails?

Barely noticeable at first, MONA *begins to stir. As they speak,
she slowly sits up.*

GEORGIE: Lying to.

BENDER: Lyin to. Yeah. That's us kids. Lyin to.

Silence.

BENDER: Mona, she never had a chance. Born
damaged. What ya gotta understand.

GEORGIE: So who's Bobby?

Pause.

BENDER: She set fire to him. My nephew. Her boy.

Pause.

BENDER: He was playin up. She was drunk, crazy.
There's this tin of kero right there and she shuts
him up. Big splash, big laugh, comedy show. But
one flick of the lighter. And he's a candle. Eight-
year-old candle. Hard work, little fulla like that.
Can't fix him. FAS, he was. You know about it?

GEORGIE: Foetal alcohol.

BENDER: Just doin the same thing over and over.
Coulda killed him myself if I'd had to deal with
it day and night, but I wasn't there. Out the
wheatbelt, workin. Time I found out, Bobby's
buried and she's locked up.

GEORGIE: Gaol.

BENDER: Nah, nuthouse.

GEORGIE: She's been discharged, released?

BENDER: She's a self-releaser. An absconder. Runs
in the family. Like the FAS. She's got it. Like I
said, brain damage. Can't learn, you know, from
ya mistakes. But she's got this idea. Somethin she
won't let go of. Why we're bloody drivin round,

campin under bridges'n sleepin in the car. You
wouldn't tell anybody, would ya? She hasn't hurt
anybody.

GEORGIE: The child—

BENDER: It was years ago. He'd be, what, near
twenty now. If he'd lived. You won't dob us in,
will you, Georgie?

GEORGIE *doesn't speak.*

BENDER: Me and Mona, we never had no certainty
like you, no safe place, no map. No magic
dreamtime rainbird. Jesus, I got no language, no
law, no bloody place. Put together from bits and
pieces, spare parts. My country's a broken-down
bus and a hundred fuckin dust farms from here
to the arse-end of Onslow. Lyin to, that's me,
all me life. All I got's bad memories and other
people's bad memories and a sister not right in
the head. I'm more fuckin lost than you ever bin
in ya life.

GEORGIE *still doesn't speak.*

BENDER: We'll be gone in the morning.

SCENE 8

Beneath the tree, the same day. MONA *has a dobro guitar on her lap. It catches the light, flashes in her face.* GEORGIE *emerges from the doorway and watches as* MONA *touches one string after another timidly before beginning to strum them all at once.*

The guitar is tuned to an open minor chord and the drone sound unlocks something in MONA. *She strums again, and she sings a note in harmony with it. She's a ruin, this poor woman with the flashing guitar, but her voice is so sad and full of longing it's somehow beautiful.*

    MONA: [*singing*] Now . . . Benny, now . . .
        Bobby . . . now? Mona now. Pa now, Mummy
        now. Now . . . Now.

And then she catches herself, sensing GEORGIE *there, turns.*

MONA: Didden mean . . . Just . . . found it.

GEORGIE: It's okay.

BENDER *emerges from the house.*

MONA: Why you cryin?

GEORGIE: Oh. Nothing. That . . . guitar, it was my husband's.

MONA *gets up.*

MONA: Everthin you touch, eh. It's them. They in it.

MONA *hands the guitar to* GEORGIE *and walks off stage right, begins to run.*

GEORGIE: Mona, it's okay. Bender?

BENDER: Where you goin?

MONA *is off.*

MONA: To the car.

Sound of the car door opening, slamming shut.

BENDER: No point gettin in there, you're not goin anywhere. Don't forget who's got the keys, Sistergirl.

GEORGIE: Think I upset her.

BENDER: Ha. Wallpaper upsets her. Sunshine, bottletops, shoelaces.

GEORGIE: So she's like the rest of us, then.

BENDER: Yeah, bloody pain in the arse. [*The sound of the Holden starting.*] Oh, Christ!

BENDER *sprints off followed by* GEORGIE *as the vehicle howls away in a rattling roar.* LU *emerges from the tree. It's as if he's watching history repeat itself.*

An horrific thud and the sound of breaking glass.

Birdsong reclaims the day. BENDER *strides back to the veranda followed by* GEORGIE *supporting* MONA. GEORGIE *sits* MONA *down but she struggles free and storms indoors.*

BENDER: Well, that's fucked it.

GEORGIE: Be glad she didn't make it out onto the road.

BENDER: Maybe woulda been better.

GEORGIE: You don't mean that.

BENDER: Sometimes I wonder.

GEORGIE: Mona's all you've got.

BENDER: I said sometimes.

GEORGIE: I get a chill now and then, out along
   that drive. Husband's brother rolled the ute there
   near the gate. Four of them, two little kids. They
   all died here, every one of them.

BENDER: What about that old man, the one up the
   pole?

GEORGIE: There in his bed. I spose one of them
   had to die of old age.

BENDER: Old age. Yeah, there's a luxury.

LU: [*startled, sensing something a second or two before
   the others*] No!

MONA *appears in the doorway with the shotgun. She points
it skyward. Pulls the trigger and sends a sound-cloud of birds
shrieking into the distance.*

MONA: Now. We do it now, we go down to the
   river now, no more bullshit.

MONA *lays the weapon down carefully, as if she's frightened herself as well as everyone else.* BENDER *rushes at her as if to strike her, but* MONA *hugs him.*

MONA: Please, little brother, I'll go back. I'll be good.

BENDER *looks at* GEORGIE *like a man hoping to be delivered.*

GEORGIE: What's down the river?

MONA: [*to* BENDER] The story.

BENDER: Orright.

MONA: Thass it, Bub.

BENDER: Ya see, our Pa—

MONA: He used to talk sometimes.

BENDER: Special times round the fire.

MONA: When he was feelin soft.

GEORGIE: Soft?

BENDER: Like a crab changin shell, just all of a
    sudden, like he couldn't help it, shell slidin away
    and there's just skin.

MONA: And he'd be soft.

BENDER: That's when he'd talk about a place on the river. South a bit. Down from Mogumber, along the river, halfway to the sea.

MONA: Special place for him.

BENDER: See, he was took for the Mission. Two year old.

MONA: Mum for New Norcia.

BENDER: Him for Moore River Mission.

MONA: Run away four times, he did.

BENDER: Nowhere to run, of course. Where's he gunna go? Doesn't know who he is, where he's from, where his people are; language flogged out of him. Doesn't even know what his mother looks like. So where's he go?

MONA: The river.

BENDER: After he run away they'd have dogs out, coppers lookin. So he just followed the river, miles and miles, stayed in the water, creepin long the bank every day, little bit, hidin. It was good country down here them days when it still rained and we had all the proper seasons.

MONA: There was roos—

BENDER: Emu—

MONA: Goanna—

BENDER: Fish to eat.

MONA: But them wadjela—

BENDER: Whitefulla cockies, they dob you in,
quick smart – farmers rather have a dingo
down the paddock than some runaway boong
from the Mission. But not this place, not this
fulla.

MONA: Big bend in the river.

BENDER: Lotsa trees, tuarts, marris, rivergums.

MONA: And some angel-man livin up a pole in
the sky.

LU: Angel, my arse.

BENDER: Never could tell what he was doin
up there.

GEORGIE: There's books about it in the house.

LU: Simeon Stylites, the pole-sitting saint.
Pilgrims'd come to see him parked up in the air.
Thirty-seven years.

GEORGIE: Like a vigil.

LU: Like a love-struck possum.

GEORGIE: Some kind of gesture.

LU: To irritate the neighbours, to piss my
mother off.

BENDER: Well, this old whitefulla – he knew
someone was camped down there, by the water.

MONA: Bet he didn't know it was a little boy.

LU: Of course he knew. He knew all about the
Mission. They all did.

BENDER: Pa camped under a overhang on the
bank. Sandy beach, couple tree branches strung
over a log. Good hiding spot. Had a fire at night,
right down low. But you'd see it flashin up the
trees, wouldn't ya. Some mornins there'd be a tin
of flour up on the bank.

MONA: Matches, melons.

BENDER: Beefsteak once.

MONA: T-bone beefsteak.

BENDER: Proper human man, he said.

MONA: Proper human man.

LU: He was entertaining himself.

BENDER: And one time the coppers come.
There was a warnin shot from up the house.

MONA: Two barrels, four-ten shotgun.

BENDER: To let him know, see, give him time.

LU: He didn't really care about blackfellas. He just
hated the government.

BENDER: And Pa, he gets his stuff, his flourbag
and billy and bit of tucker and he swims it across
the river, buries it, and when they come, those
wallopers and their dogs, he's across the bend, in
the reeds, like a sweetwater turtle, just—

MONA: Eyes up.

BENDER: Watchin, till they go. Course he always
got caught in the end. But it was other farms,

other whitefullas did him in. Not here, not this
old fulla.

LU: You can't make a hero out of a man like
that. Maybe he didn't dob anyone in, but he
knew what they were doing to those kids at
Mogumber; people knew.

BENDER: But here. If this is really the place.

MONA: I can feel it, Bub.

BENDER: Made it his country. Lying there locked
in the barracks at night. Nowhere that's home
unless he lets it be the Mission and he isn't gunna
let it be the Mission he calls country. So all he's
got's this one riverbend. Comin back to him in
his mind. For years. All his life. Singin it up in
his head, like some kind of—

MONA: Paradise.

BENDER: If he really was here.

MONA: Carn, Bub.

BENDER: I dunno.

MONA: [*to* GEORGIE] Scared, him.

GEORGIE: Scared of what?

BENDER: Nothin.

MONA: Thassit. Scared there's nothin. Here, Bub. I'll look after ya. Didn't I look after ya?

MONA *takes his arm, gestures for* GEORGIE *to accompany them.* BENDER *relents.*

Light softens about them, shimmering a moment.

SCENE 9

At the edge of the paddock in the late afternoon sun, BENDER, MONA *and* GEORGIE *stand looking down into the parched riverbed. As they speak* LU *comes down behind them.*

MONA: Ahh. Look.

BENDER: Down from the bridge.

MONA: Long paddock west.

BENDER: Big bend right here.

MONA: This the place.

BENDER: He really was here?

LU: Yes.

MONA: Too right. I can feel it. I can see it real.

BENDER: It's enough. Knowin that.

MONA: It's good.

BENDER: Yeah.

GEORGIE: Did he ever come back?

BENDER: Never could.

MONA: Scared. Like him, here. Scared it wasn't real, that he'd have nothin.

BENDER: Reckon so.

MONA: Don't be scared no more, Bub. See? Pa's here in the warm yeller sand, cookin bream on the fire, river flowin past, birds all round, free and safe. Them balgas, them grasstrees up, that mooja, that Christmas tree out, all golden flowers out, heavy orange flowers just fallin on your head like gold. Sunshine gold. Pollen gold. Fallin on Pa, on Clancy, on William, on Mummy, on you Benderboy.

BENDER *lays a hand tenderly on his sister's head. And golden-yellow blossoms fall from the sky onto* MONA's *ashen head.*

BENDER: And Bobby.

MONA: True? Really?

BENDER: Aw, yeah.

MONA: Yellow flower dust, like sunshine?

BENDER: That's right.

MONA: They here.

BENDER: That's right. All of 'em.

GEORGIE: All of them?

LU: All of them.

LU *hovers behind them, wants to touch these people, his wife. But refrains. Sits by them, stares into the river of their memories, of their story, their vision until the sound of water begins to purl and gurgle.*

GEORGIE: But it's dry. And everything's dying.

MONA: Nah. Just dreamin of rain. Like one thirsty woman. Lyin awake, thinkin of water. Everythin singin for rain. To make it real, just from wanting.

BENDER: Like you, Sis.

MONA: Like Pa.

BENDER: Them stories.

MONA: Bub, we in the story now.

GEORGIE *steps off a little way to give them space.* LU *comes close to* GEORGIE. *She senses him.*

GEORGIE: It wasn't a mistake. Coming here with you.

LU: The weirdo and his prickly girlfriend, planting olives.

GEORGIE: In the alkaline dirt, above the river, in the days when there was still rain.

LU: Early years there was enough to keep the saplings up.

GEORGIE: But after that they were on their own.

LU: They found the water down deep.

GEORGIE: Good trees.

LU: Good fruit.

GEORGIE: Lovely lovely oil.

LU: Should have planted natives.

GEORGIE: Scrub?

LU: Scrub is what you call vegetation you don't understand.

GEORGIE: Well, you can thank your mother for the olives.

LU: I do. Did.

GEORGIE: All those years expecting you to drown, for God's sake! And I come out and there you are.

LU: Watching the sky inhale the clouds and the birds, like the last warm air from my lungs—

GEORGIE: Lying on the dirt, smiling, like a five-year-old who's finally caught the ball.

LU: All those dragonflies riding the updraughts.

GEORGIE: Under the house tree.

LU: Of all the trees. The first she planted.

GEORGIE: Smiling. Making me a widow. It was . . . incomprehensible. Ridiculous.

LU: But it felt calm, love . . . fair.

GEORGIE: It was good, wasn't it? Us?

LU: Yes, love. It was good.

GEORGIE: I want it all again.

LU: It's always here.

GEORGIE: Did I make you happy?

LU: Mate, I couldn't believe my luck.

GEORGIE: And now there's none of you left.

LU: Not true. Dust. Ash. Still here. All of us. Stubborn bugger, the olive. Once the roots are down. Hard as a story, tough as a song.

LU *retreats to his tree.*

GEORGIE: As a song.

GEORGIE *leaves the others by the bank as the light begins to fade toward dusk.*

MONA: Seen it. Him in the water, in the reeds, eyes out like a turtle.

BENDER: Yup.

MONA: Save ya pennies, boy. Come back, we buy this place.

BENDER: That's a lotta dead cats, Sis.

MONA: When we's sleepin under that bridge. I knew.

BENDER: Too right.

MONA: Didden believe me.

BENDER: True. But you could feel it.

MONA: Feel him. Yeah.

BENDER: Done good.

MONA: Ay. Done rool good.

Crickets herald the night.

SCENE 10

The veranda that evening. GEORGIE, MONA *and* BENDER
sit on the step gazing out into the hot darkness. MONA's *brief*
period of lucidity has passed. She rocks and fidgets, paying only
occasional attention.

GEORGIE: I was thinking of heading into town
    tomorrow, do some shopping. You need
    anything?

BENDER: We'll be gone.

GEORGIE: Gone? What about the carbie?
    The radiator, the tyre, the headlight?

BENDER: Bit of fence-wire, she'll be right.

GEORGIE *is stunned, unable to process this news.*

BENDER: Your husband. Gone, isn't he? Like, permanent?

GEORGIE: Six weeks.

BENDER: Shot through?

GEORGIE: Died.

BENDER: Oh.

GEORGIE: There in the yard.

BENDER: Oh!

GEORGIE: Yes.

BENDER: I'm . . . sorry. Heart attack, was it?

GEORGIE: Broke his neck.

BENDER: Jesus.

GEORGIE: You think you see your own death?

BENDER: You talkin personal or general? Cause—

GEORGIE: In general.

BENDER: Generally I'd take dyin personal. Where'd they bury him?

GEORGIE: Well. They didn't.

BENDER: Some people the crematin sort.

GEORGIE: Not him.

BENDER: So . . .

GEORGIE: I buried him, myself.

BENDER: You what?

He looks out across the moonlit paddocks.

GEORGIE: True story.

BENDER: Isn't that . . . illegal? Isn't there a rule?

GEORGIE: Lu wasn't very big on rules.

BENDER: You mean you dug a hole and buried him
    yourself?

GEORGIE: Took me two days.

BENDER: Jesus. Where?

GEORGIE *tilts her head toward the river.*

MONA: Not the river.

GEORGIE: No, the other side.

BENDER: Dragged him—

GEORGIE: Drove him! Had to put him on the backseat.

BENDER: Across the river, what's there?

GEORGIE: Some limestone pinnacles. He had a thing about them. Besides, the sand's softer there; it's easier to dig.

BENDER: I'll be buggered. And no one knows?

GEORGIE *shakes her head.*

BENDER: But . . . won't they come lookin?

GEORGIE: Who?

BENDER: Someone always knows. Gov'ment.

GEORGIE: No phone, no credit cards, no paperwork; didn't vote, didn't pay tax. He was invisible. Even his vehicles are unregistered. I used to think it was mad, but maybe it was genius.

BENDER: But in the district?

GEORGIE: Like his dad, a – weirdo. No one comes here.

BENDER: But people must see him come and go.

GEORGIE: But he goes off all the time, gone – *pff* – normal.

BENDER: And, what, it's your place now? Cause you're married. That's one bit of paper.

GEORGIE: Well, actually . . .

BENDER: You weren't married.

GEORGIE: Not on paper.

BENDER: So you got no . . .

GEORGIE: Title, no.

They share a moment's mutual recognition.

BENDER: Still, people like you always get good lawyers, you'll be right.

GEORGIE: Bit awkward. Especially with a body on the premises.

BENDER: Right.

GEORGIE: So here we are. All of us.

BENDER: No paper. No title.

BENDER *looks at* MONA *but she's lost the thread. And a fresh thought occurs to him.*

BENDER: Listen, how's a fulla get a broken neck out here?

GEORGIE: There was a kite.

BENDER: A kite? A kite broke his neck?

GEORGIE: Up in the tree; it was all tangled, line and everything. Been there for days. Don't even know where it came from, just drifted in on the southerly, but he wanted to get it down, said it made him sad to see it up there like a wounded bird in a snare, flapping away in the hot wind.

He points to the kite on the wall.

BENDER: Not that one?

GEORGIE: Same one. He slipped, fell. I came out, and there he was.

BENDER: True?

GEORGIE: True.

BENDER: Doesn't look like a fulla gunna be killed by a kite.

GEORGIE: How do you know what he looks like?

BENDER: Seen the photos.

GEORGIE: You went through my photos?

BENDER: I was lookin for something else.

GEORGIE: Like, a screwdriver? Ice cream?

MONA: [*stirring*] Ice cream?

BENDER: Not a bad lookin fulla.

GEORGIE: No. Not bad at all.

BENDER: And you buried him?

GEORGIE: I did.

BENDER: And kept the kite that killed him.

GEORGIE: Yes.

BENDER: Jesus, and you reckon the men're eccentric.

GEORGIE: Bender, I'm thinking of buying my own press.

BENDER: Good luck to ya.

GEORGIE: What's the point of growing olives and selling them on for a pittance if you can press them yourself? Triple the money – more.

BENDER: Wouldn't know.

GEORGIE: I'll sell the boat, all the gear. There's sixty, seventy thousand dollars' worth.

BENDER: What? With no papers?

GEORGIE: People round here, Bender, they're not too zealous about documentation. I think it'll work. I think we can hang on.

BENDER: We?

GEORGIE: Well.

BENDER: That's a lotta money to blow on farm machinery when it hasn't rained in five years.

GEORGIE: There's birds aren't there? If there are
   birds the world is still alive. I think it'll work.

BENDER: You been drinkin?

MONA: Fuckin have not.

GEORGIE: Come on, you know a bit about machines.

BENDER: Some. Not college, no ticket. Don't know
   anythin about olive presses. Just passin through.
   We'll be gone in the mornin.

GEORGIE: But you've said that every—

BENDER: And I'm telling you—

GEORGIE: But I'm asking, offering—

BENDER: What, why?

GEORGIE: Why not? You have as much right to
   be here as I do.

MONA *gets up, growling, she heads inside.*

MONA: Goin to bed. Bloody head hurts!

GEORGIE: Bender, you've got nowhere to go,
   and what about Mona?

BENDER: Have to go back, eventually.

GEORGIE: Send her back? Listen to yourself!
    She's safe here. Sanctuary, Bender.

BENDER: Why're you even stayin? What's here
    for ya?

GEORGIE: Family. Stories. I dunno. Spare parts.

BENDER: Can't sit around here rest of me life
    waitin for it to rain.

GEORGIE: Why not? It's not raining anywhere else.

BENDER: And I'm sposed to stay, for you? Cause
    you're lonely?

GEORGIE: I took you in.

BENDER: I don't even know you.

GEORGIE: Mona's right, you're just scared.

BENDER: Why you talkin like this?

GEORGIE: Sometimes the shell comes off.

BENDER: Arghh.

GEORGIE: Please. Just think about it.

BENDER: Got a head like a kicked bucket.
    I gotta go to bed. I can't think anymore.

BENDER *leaves and* GEORGIE *is left with the mournful,
questioning call of the owl.*

SCENE 11

Cockatoos herald the light of morning. MONA emerges onto the veranda, sits at the table and begins to eat cereal noisily. Leaning from the window, BENDER nurses a cup of tea as birds riot about outside. GEORGIE emerges from the doorway, surveys them, pensively.

BENDER: Mona. Shut your mouth.

MONA: [*with a full mouth*] Didden say nothin!

BENDER: When you eat. Shut your mouth when you're chewin, it's disgustin.

MONA: Jesus! Can't drink, can't eat!

GEORGIE: Leave her alone, she's alright.

BENDER: Who asked ya?

GEORGIE: Grumpy bugger.

MONA: Yair!

BENDER: Christ, a man's surrounded.

GEORGIE: What side of the bed you get out of this morning?

BENDER: No side. Couldn't sleep.

GEORGIE: Everything orright?

MONA: Thinkin, thinkin. Tossin, turnin, fartin, snorin.

BENDER: Quit naggin me, woman.

MONA: Not a mornin person, him.

GEORGIE *laughs.*

BENDER: Give over, both of yez.

GEORGIE: Surrounded! By an army of two women!

The women laugh. BENDER *cracks. He snatches the kite from where it hangs on the wall.*

MONA: Mad bugger. Bad manners!

GEORGIE: What are you doing?

He crosses the yard, pauses with the kite a moment and lets them hang a long moment:

BENDER: See if this bloody thing'll fly.

BLACKOUT. MUSIC.

Production Notes

Signs of Life was first produced by the Black Swan State Theatre Company. It premiered at the Albany Entertainment Centre on 16 July 2012 and toured regional centres, including Esperance, Merredin, Margaret River, Mandurah, Geraldton, Tom Price, Paraburdoo and Moora. In July and August it was performed in the Heath Ledger Theatre at the State Theatre Centre, Perth.

CAST AND CREW

GEORGIE	Helen Morse
BENDER	Tom E. Lewis
MONA	Pauline Whyman
LU FOX	George Shevtsov
DIRECTOR	Kate Cherry
SET & COSTUME DESIGNER	Zoe Atkinson
LIGHTING DESIGNER	Jon Buswell
SOUND DESIGNER/COMPOSER	Ben Collins
ASSISTANT DIRECTOR	Damon Lockwood
PRODUCTION MANAGER	Garry Ferguson
STAGE MANAGER	Erin Coubrough

The DIRT MUSIC story continues!

BLACK SWAN STATE THEATRE COMPANY
AND SYDNEY THEATRE COMPANY PRESENT

Signs of Life

BY TIM WINTON

FROM **21** JUL | UNTIL **18** AUG

STATE THEATRE
CENTRE OF WA

Signs of Life is proudly part of the 2012 City of Perth Winter Arts Season

SYDNEY THEATRE CO

FEATURING
Tom E. Lewis
Helen Morse
George Sheutsou
Pauline Whyman

DIRECTOR
Kate Cherry

SET & COSTUME DESIGNER
Zoe Atkinson

LIGHTING DESIGNER
Jon Buswell

SOUND DESIGNER/ COMPOSER
Ben Collins

ASSISTANT DIRECTOR
Damon Lockwood

black swan
STATE THEATRE COMPANY
www.bsstc.com.au

Book @ BOCS 9484 1133 or www.bocsticketing.com.au

mix94.5   The West Australian   WorleyParsons   WATER   ANZ   RioTinto

From 2 November–22 December 2012 the Sydney Theatre Company co-production ran in The Playhouse at the Sydney Opera House.

CAST AND CREW

GEORGIE	Heather Mitchell
BENDER	Aaron Pedersen
MONA	Pauline Whyman
LU FOX	George Shevtsov
DIRECTOR	Kate Cherry
SET & COSTUME DESIGNER	Zoe Atkinson
LIGHTING DESIGNER	Jon Buswell
SOUND DESIGNER/COMPOSER	Ben Collins
FIGHT DIRECTOR	Scott Witt
ASSISTANT DIRECTOR	Damon Lockwood
VOICE & TEXT COACH	Charmian Gradwell
PRODUCTION MANAGER	John Colvin
ASSISTANT STAGE MANAGER	Victoria Marques
REHEARSAL PHOTOGRAPHY	Grant Sparkes-Carroll
PRODUCTION PHOTOGRAPHY	Lisa Tomasetti

SYDNEY THEATRE CO

Sydney Theatre Company,
Black Swan State Theatre Company and
Commonwealth Bank present

A NEW PLAY BY
TIM WINTON
SIGNS OF LIFE

The dead watch over
the living as the *Dirt Music*
story continues

2 NOV – 22 DEC 2012
SYDNEY OPERA HOUSE

WITH
HEATHER MITCHELL
AARON PEDERSEN
GEORGE SHEVTSOV
PAULINE WHYMAN

DIRECTOR
KATE CHERRY
DESIGNER
ZOE ATKINSON

LIGHTING DESIGNER
JON BUSWELL
COMPOSER & SOUND DESIGNER
BEN COLLINS

SYDNEYTHEATRE.COM.AU 9250 1777
SYDNEYOPERAHOUSE.COM 9250 1700

black swan
STATE THEATRE COMPANY

CommonwealthBank ◆
PRESENTING SPONSOR

ASSOCIATE SPONSOR

Australian Government

NSW | Trade &
Investment
Arts NSW

Mona (Pauline Whyman) and Bender (Tom E. Lewis)

Georgie (Helen Morse) and Lu (George Shevtsov)

Bender (Tom E. Lewis), Georgie (Helen Morse) and Mona (Pauline Whyman)

Lu (George Shevtsov) and Mona (Pauline Whyman)

Bender (Tom E. Lewis)

Bender (Aaron Pedersen) and Georgie (Heather Mitchell)

Director's Note

On the surface *Signs of Life* is a simple story. Two strangers in distress arrive at a farmhouse in the wheatbelt late at night. A woman is there, on the veranda of the farmhouse, frightened, alone. She greets the interlopers with a series of questions.

What has brought these people together? What do they have in common? Why does a dried up river matter to all of them? These questions hang over the play. As the seemingly gentle story unfolds, we realise the depth of Tim Winton's vision. The play tackles deep questions of identity, sustainability and community without ever offering easy answers.

The woman on the veranda is Georgie. As readers of *Dirt Music* already know, Georgie is from a well-off middle-class family and although she has been transplanted to a hard rural life, she retains a sense of security, an understanding of her place in the world, only challenged by a loss that occurs before the beginning of the play. When strangers intrude on her sanctuary, in a potentially threatening situation, Georgie overcomes her terror and offers compassion and generosity. Georgie is resilient, adaptable and articulate. In the face of loss and sorrow, Georgie is willing to navigate her way through unknown territory with nothing to rely on but instinct and daring.

The interlopers are Bender and his sister, Mona. Ironically, Bender has the least sense of place; although he longs to identify with the landscape he is also terrified of its power. He has no traditional language and no real sense of belonging, but he has a profound sense of family – a dedication to his addled sister despite his horror and revulsion at her past. Like Georgie, Bender understands that potent narratives and our relationship with our landscape shape our sense of self and offer us the possibility of healing.

We chose to set the play in a psychic landscape; the farmhouse is an island of loneliness, safety and solitude, inhabited by ghosts and memories. The past has a very powerful hold over the characters in the present, as ghosts interweave effortlessly with the present and claim their reckoning. The ghost of Lu embodies the power of the past. At times, memories seem more potent than the present. Georgie, Bender and Mona cannot inhabit the present with any peace or clarity until they revisit and name their past.

A surprising journey towards mutual respect unfolds as Bender and Georgie form an unlikely alliance. Out of mutual distrust comes surprising understanding. Bender, Mona and Georgie are all damaged, but none of them accept being defined as victims. Only when they face their fears and go to the river, can they experience the potency of storytelling and the wonderment of transformation.

Bringing a new Australian play to life is always a unique journey and a great privilege for the Company. As Socrates said, 'The unexamined life is not worth living.' Tim's play, full of mystery and grace, reminds us of the potency of those lines, offering us the opportunity as Australians to understand ourselves and our amazing landscape better. I could not ask for a finer collaborator. Thank you Tim, Helen, George, Tom, Pauline, Aaron, Heather, Damon, Ben, Zoe and Jon for collaborating on a journey that celebrates finding signs of life in unexpected places.

Kate Cherry
Director

Helen Morse as Georgie and
George Shevtsov as Lu in rehearsal

Piano at Ross Bolleter's ruined piano sanctuary

Shrine

Contents

A beach house above a rocky headland on the south coast of Western Australia. Nearby is a roadside shrine at the edge of a karri forest.

CHARACTERS

ADAM MANSFIELD	a retired vigneron and property developer
MARY MANSFIELD	a businesswoman
JACK MANSFIELD	(19) their dead son
JUNE FENTON	(19) a local cellarhand
BEN	(20) Jack's former friend
WILL	(20) Jack's former friend

June (Whitney Richards)

SCENE I

A roadside shrine at the edge of a forest. Lights up on a man scraping furiously at a large tree with a pocketknife. The latticed light gradually reveals him freshening a great wound in the tree's trunk. At its base stands a white cross festooned with beer cans, bourbon bottles and an advertising placard that reads: JACK LIVES HERE.

> ADAM: Sometimes I wish there'd been blood. Something left behind. Sick, I know, but a stain on the ground, maybe there'd be comfort in it. A man could indulge himself in a bit of nature romance – blood, soil, presence – all that mystic nonsense. But there was hardly a mark on you. Nothing to show but a scar on a tree.

He snaps the knife shut and kicks over the cross and all its decorations.

SCENE 2

A bolt of light reveals MARY *and* ADAM *beside a hospital gurney upon which their son* JACK *lies dead.*

MARY: It isn't right.

ADAM: No, it doesn't look right.

MARY: Don't tell me he looks peaceful. Don't you dare!

ADAM: Mary.

MARY: Is it him? Is this still him?

ADAM: I don't know.

MARY: Unblemished.

ADAM: The impact.

MARY: Trauma – they said the word as if they knew
what it meant, what it actually felt like.

ADAM: You just couldn't see the damage. His
organs all adrift within him.

MARY: Not a mark.

ADAM: Momentum makes us superhuman.

MARY: Angelic.

ADAM: You fly. There you are, flying. And inside
half a second you're not even human anymore.
You're just meat.

MARY: Don't.

ADAM: I expected him to be so much lighter. Gone,
they said. He slipped away. Like a thought.

MARY: Couldn't hold him. Couldn't lift him. He
was so cold and heavy.

ADAM: That's the thing. By the time we drove
down – Christ, or did we fly? By the time we
got there he'd been refrigerated. Or maybe I
imagined that. I expected a boy and there he was,

a man, so heavy, so solid he seemed . . . plausible.
And despite the stink of antiseptic it did smell
like him.

MARY: Lanolin. Coconut.

ADAM: That sweet scent they put in surfboard wax
these days.

MARY: No. That's the smell of a girl.

ADAM: Standing there in the little mortuary room,
I kept asking myself, Is this our son?

MARY: Why won't he speak? I can't bear it.

ADAM: And she's looking at me like I'm a stranger.

MARY: Adam is silent. A monument to his own
dignity. Can't stand it another moment. So I run.

ADAM: The bloke says, 'Is this your son?'

MARY: Bolted. Blind. Just a mad creature. Trolleys,
locked doors, glass threaded with wire I try to
sieve myself through.

ADAM: 'This?' I say. Thinking: It looks like him.
Is this Jack or just the stuff that made him
possible? A body's just the plant and equipment,

not the enterprise itself.

MARY: I'm trapped, hurling myself against the walls and windows to get free.

ADAM: Smiling, they said. Smiling. But I can't see it.

MARY: Until everything goes blank.

ADAM: Nothing.

MARY: Cold and dark.

ADAM: The bloke's talking to me. Fella with a clipboard and a lab coat like some consultant flown in to oversee the vintage.

MARY: I come to and I'm on the floor. Feet and legs all round me – not Adam's. He's oblivious, still in there scratching his chin, holding himself together.

ADAM: 'Mister Mansfield?' he says.

MARY: Arms and soft hands. Crooning voices, soft and kind. But nothing to console me because I want Adam. I want him to haul me out of the white, shiny horror I've slipped into.

ADAM: 'Is this your son?'

MARY: And I'm broken. Completely. Knew I'd keep
breaking forever.

ADAM: 'Yes,' I say. 'Yes, this is my son. This is Jack
Mansfield.'

MARY: Like a man unbroken, unbreakable.

ADAM: And I sign for him. Take delivery of the
facts.

MARY: The end.

Mary (Sarah McNeill) and Jack (Paul Ashcroft)

SCENE 3

The roadside shrine. Enter JUNE *who surveys the shrine in disarray. As she speaks* JACK *is revealed nearby, watching on.*

JUNE: Fucksake! Again . . .

She stoops to collect the scattered bits and pieces and begins to reassemble the shrine.

JUNE: Least I'll remember.

JACK: Strange that it should make a difference.

JUNE: Weird how you can see the Point from here. That white flash – see? – the wave breakin on the end. Wonder if it's any kind of comfort, havin it right there, close by. I know you loved it. Remember your big white smile all those

mornins, runnin down to the water with your
board.

JACK: Remembering, June. It's not like a job or
anything.

JUNE: I'll never forget. I can't.

JACK: I know.

JUNE: Hardly imagine it all now, hardly believe it.

JACK: It was half a day. Barely that.

JUNE: Not even a whole night. But the whole sea,
that's what we had.

JACK: Barely a moment.

JUNE: We must have been out of our minds.

SCENE 4

The beach house. ADAM *stands at the window, a little drunk.*

>   ADAM: God, will you look at that. A sea mist.
>   Rolling up the headland, hanging over the
>   paddocks like a promise. How's a man account
>   for that wanton bit of beauty? The cold, dark,
>   pitiless ocean giving off a vapour so benign. In a
>   world so utterly bereft of promise. Christ man,
>   listen to yourself!

*He turns from the window, crosses the room and pulls out
another bottle. He consults the label.*

>   ADAM: 'North-facing slopes, maritime air, and red
>   karri gravel: such are the building blocks of the
>   wine we call Ocean Ridge.' Wrote that before
>   the first vines even went in – there's confidence.

He opens the bottle, pours himself a measure, swirls it, sniffs it and fills his glass. After such aesthetic ritual, drinks the wine off in one bovine gulp.

ADAM: When you're young you make things happen just by thinking of them. If you want them enough. Provided you've done your homework. Least that's what you tell yourself, what you tell him when he comes home with his schoolboy tales of woe.

As he speaks JUNE *appears at the door.*

JUNE: Sorry.

ADAM: Fuck me running!

JUNE: Sorry?

ADAM: I . . . I beg your pardon, love. I wasn't expecting anyone.

JUNE: Didn't mean to creep up on ya. Well, actually that's not true – I *was* creepin up. Sorry.

ADAM: Do we know each other?

JUNE: Um, well, I know you, of course, Mister Mansfield. Ah, I'm June?

ADAM: June.

JUNE: Ocean Ridge. The winery. It's just—

ADAM: I know where it is. I own it.

JUNE: I know.

ADAM: Well, used to own it.

JUNE: I know.

ADAM: I didn't hear a vehicle. How'd you get here, June?

JUNE: Parked out on the beach road. Gate's locked.

ADAM: Which traditionally means something. What'd you say your name was?

JUNE: June.

ADAM: Family name?

JUNE: I used to pick for you. Started when I was at school, when it was just sheds. Cellarhand now.

ADAM: What name?

JUNE: Fenton.

ADAM: Oh. Right.

JUNE: My dad—

ADAM: I know.

JUNE: Yeah, everyone knows.

ADAM: And no one's holding it against you.

JUNE: Nah, that'd never happen. Not in this town.

ADAM: Fenton.

JUNE: Says it all, doesn't it.

ADAM: So, we're old colleagues, then. Comrades at arms. Fellow toilers in the field.

JUNE: Ah, whatever you reckon.

ADAM: Well, June, you gave me quite a fright, there. No harm done. Anyway, I'm off.

JUNE: Where?

ADAM: Well, Perth. Told the missus I'd be home today. And I hate to be on the road after dark.

JUNE: Roos.

ADAM: That, and I start to see things.

JUNE: Not worth the stress, is it?

ADAM: Seeing things?

JUNE: Worryin. Drivin in the dark, dodgin animals.

ADAM: Yes. No.

JUNE: You're in real estate.

ADAM: Yes, in quite a state – you're rather observant, June – but this is me on a good day.

JUNE: That's not what I said, what I meant.

ADAM: I know what you meant, I heard what you said.

JUNE: I'm sorry.

ADAM: And yes, I was, in my way, in real estate. Property developer. Let's just say I retired hurt from that game.

JUNE: You went broke?

ADAM: Lost interest.

JUNE: Last year.

ADAM: Yes, you could say I failed to develop.

JUNE: Why'd you sell the winery?

ADAM: You know, I can't even remember. Honest
to God.

JUNE: Must've hurt, lettin it go.

ADAM: Yes, I suppose it must've. Bit of a blur, that.

JUNE: I . . . we couldn't believe it.

ADAM: Divestment, June. Sounds rather rational
and precise, doesn't it? Well, it wasn't. But here
I am, free and clear. Free. And clear.

He turns as if preparing to leave, but he's a little lost.

JUNE: So, what d'you do all day?

ADAM: Do?

JUNE: God, I'm sorry, that's rude. I'm so stupid.

ADAM: Not at all. Perfectly reasonable question.
And by the time I reach the outskirts of the
city I'm sure I'll have come up with a plausible

answer. But don't hold your breath.

JUNE: I just wanted to say how sorry, what a terrible thing.

ADAM: Listen, what're they doing to the sav blanc? It's . . .

JUNE: What?

ADAM: Flabby, sweet.

JUNE: Too slow gettin it off. Too many cooks, you know?

ADAM: Well, it's their funeral.

Adam (John Howard) and June (Whitney Richards)

SCENE 5

Each in their own pool of merciless light, ADAM *and* MARY *stand separated by a gulf of dark space.*

MARY: The funeral is its own exquisite indignity.

ADAM: All of them there. Every name on the database – school, business, sport. Jack's friends. People you've never seen before in your life. I stand there and suck it up, every platitude, every Olympian feat of insincerity, every well-meant banality, religious and secular, every Hallmark moment.

MARY: In flames.

ADAM: Taking it, just taking it.

MARY: I'm on fire. Tongues of fire from my head, ears, mouth, streaming from the ends of my fingers.

ADAM: Just getting through it, sucking it up. Until the moment the coffin slides away through the velvet curtain.

MARY: And I feel it, pure and horrible, strong as the shock of pushing him free.

ADAM: She starts screaming. Falls down like a headscarfed immigrant, beating her hands on the floor. Jesus, we've got everything but the blood-curdling ululation. The moaning and yowling, it's . . . it's . . . awful. Bovine. Frightening.

MARY: Like making him. Feeling him live outside me.

ADAM: And after that, where do you go? Within a week the fridge is all festering leftovers, casseroles you'll never eat, mornays that have graduated from unappealing to genuinely hazardous. And the living room's a dead zone at the silent heart of a house suddenly too big and ostentatious.

MARY: Empty. Curtains drawn. Separate rooms. Nothing.

ADAM: Nothing but thinking it through and over, chewing at it, knowing this . . . this . . . this box of ash should be someone else's.

MARY: The poison runs up your spine. I lie in bed and feel it seep and pulse.

ADAM: And of course you can't say it, but the truth is you want the other two dead.

MARY: His mates.

ADAM: Them for him.

MARY: Smarmy Ben, sleazy Will.

ADAM: He was twice the man either'll ever be.

MARY: Bastards.

ADAM: Can't say I ever liked them.

MARY: Never did buy their neat little story.

ADAM: They were full of food and booze, from my fridge, my cellar.

MARY: Reeking.

ADAM: The cops said it.

MARY: Stank of it.

ADAM: And Jack was sober.

MARY: Took blood. Adam insisted.

ADAM: Clear his name.

MARY: Blood. From his unblemished body.

ADAM: I bought him that little car.

MARY: Gave him the keys the day he finished
school and not a moment before.

ADAM: I mean, how wild can you go in a Corolla,
for pity's sake? Engine like a sewing machine.
Had an airbag.

MARY: Not a mark on him.

ADAM: But that bend. Day or night, it wouldn't
take much to come unglued there. Cops said
it could happen to anybody. Which is of no
consolation whatsoever when they're covered
in blood and alive and he's out there in the wet
bracken, pure and whole and slowly dying inside.

MARY: Why couldn't it have been them? It should
have been them.

ADAM: We're not bad people, not reckless. Hands on the tiller. All due diligence. This sort of thing doesn't happen to people like us. She goes to pieces, poor devil. I can feel her glower at me through a closed door – through all the closed doors. So what can I do? One of us has to keep it together. Best to keep mum. No knowing what you might say, is there? Christ, the wounded banalities you could utter. Who needs to hear that shit? The shame'd kill you both.

MARY: Say something! Anything! For God's sake, speak. I can't stand it!

ADAM: You take it in silence. Like a tree. Silent, shivering, soaking up the impact.

MARY: It's as if they both died, father and son. One taken, the other withdrawing, endlessly, pointlessly, bravely silent.

ADAM: And then, incredibly, a year passes. Not long after that it's his birthday. You've quit the firm, sold off the winery, and the weekend trips go from quarterly to monthly and then every fortnight, until you're gone as often as you're home because even you can't bear yourself silent in her presence, can't stand your mighty, courageous self-control. She won't come down here.

MARY: I don't want to go there.

ADAM: But you love the beach house.

MARY: I don't want to drive past that tree.

ADAM: But when we're together, neither of us is really present. It's . . . bloody frightening. You keep up the serve-and-volley. Your bodies are there. But there's nothing in it, no connection, no fellow-feeling. Love? Yes, that old, quiet, bone-murdering ache, that's there, but it's—

MARY: Unbearable.

ADAM: I watch those kids out there rolling down the Point like seals, barely even conscious that I'm looking for him – you silly twat – scanning the water for the broad triangle of him sat up in his wetsuit. Alive, laughing, seething with thoughtless youth, the future still trundling at him like all those waves spilling in from across the horizon. How bloody stupid is that?

SCENE 6

The beach house the same night. ADAM *stands transfixed in thought.* JUNE *watches him slowly return to the moment.*

ADAM: Jesus, you're soaked.

JUNE: It's nothin.

ADAM: I'm sorry, I didn't even notice. Get that coat off. Come stand by the fire.

JUNE *hesitates, then wriggles out of her coat and wrings her beanie over the hearth.* ADAM *brings her a towel and watches her dry off until they both feel self-conscious. He fetches a bottle and two glasses. Pours her a glass and proffers it.*

ADAM: The tempranillo.

JUNE *looks in vain for somewhere to hang the coat, the beanie, the towel. She takes the wine, juggling all her burdens, examines it for colour and clarity, swirls it around the glass, sniffs it. She takes a sip, sluices it impressively around her mouth and then abruptly spits it back into the glass.*

ADAM: Yes, well, I was against the planting.

JUNE: It's good, but.

ADAM: Yeah, you look enthusiastic.

JUNE: Nah, it's gunna work.

ADAM: So why'd you gob it up so quick?

JUNE: Well, I don't really drink wine.

ADAM: So why am I asking your opinion? Jesus.

JUNE: But it's good fruit. Structure's there.

JUNE *wipes her mouth indelicately and settles for dumping her wet clothes in a heap. She sets her glass back on the table. ADAM is agitated, all at sea.*

ADAM: Well, there's whisky.

JUNE: I'm fine.

ADAM: Something to warm you up.

JUNE: Milo?

ADAM: Milo?

JUNE: Sorry.

ADAM: There isn't any Milo.

JUNE: There used to be.

ADAM *has a half-hearted look in the pantry. And finds a tin of Milo.*

ADAM: Well, I'll be damned. I'll . . . the kettle.

JUNE *moves to the window and surveys the bay.*

ADAM: Wild out there.

JUNE: Yeah, it's rough.

ADAM: Some days you thank God you're not a
    sailor, eh?

JUNE: I spose.

ADAM: Storm like that, the swell, the ugly confused
    sea, the gale forcing you in against the cliffs.

Nowhere safe to put in. Night falling. It'd be
purgatory.

JUNE: I . . . I guess.

ADAM: Horrible.

JUNE: I guess.

ADAM: Thoughts like that really cheer me up.

JUNE: What?

ADAM *takes up the glass she's left on his table and drinks it off
in a gulp.* JUNE *reacts with dismay. She can't decide if he's so
drunk he doesn't remember that she's spat in it or if he's done it
to unnerve her. Either way she's rattled. Unable to disguise how
much he's enjoying himself,* ADAM *pours her a mug of Milo
and brings it to her.*

ADAM: So. You don't drink my wine.

JUNE: Any wine. It's not personal.

ADAM: Beer, I suppose. And bourbon.

JUNE: Nah. Nothin now.

ADAM *retreats a little, retrieves his own glass.*

ADAM: You're a puzzle, June.

JUNE: Cause I don't drink?

ADAM: Why would you climb over a locked gate?

JUNE: Wanted to talk to you.

ADAM: And what about me, the householder, what
about what I wanted?

JUNE: I was angry. I wasn't thinkin.

ADAM: Angry? At me? Girlie, you've still got your
job. I can buy and sell what I want. I don't have
to answer to the likes of you.

JUNE: It's not about that.

ADAM: Well, what is it?

JUNE: I was filthy 'cause ya did it again. Ya keep doin
it over and over again – I've seen ya.

ADAM: Doing what, exactly?

JUNE: You know.

ADAM: Risky thing to do in the country, June,
approach a house uninvited, where you're

probably not welcome.

JUNE: You don't need to tell me!

ADAM: Christ. Of course. I'm sorry. I'm a bit . . .
I don't know what I was thinking.

JUNE: Doesn't matter. Long time ago.

ADAM *takes a moment to regain his composure, to think past the fog of booze. He sits in an armchair and assembles himself as the man of the house.*

ADAM: So, what pressing affair did you want to see
me about? In your moment of righteous anger.

JUNE: Like I said. You. Kickin things over.

ADAM: What?

JUNE: On the highway. The bend. The cross. The
stuff. Happens every time you're down. You
knock it over. I've seen you.

ADAM: So, it's you, then. The little roadside shrine.
The beer cans, bourbon bottles, all the bogan
placards.

JUNE: You don't understand.

ADAM: Funny, June. I was picturing a Commodore, a muscle ute. Boys with stubby holders and beanies. NO FAT CHICKS sticker.

JUNE: What?

ADAM: A carload of country boys, June.

JUNE: Only the once.

ADAM: Once what?

JUNE: And they weren't country boys, neither. He didn't really know any country boys. These guys showed up in a Range Rover.

ADAM: A Range Rover?

JUNE: Brand new, with P-plates. Four boys. Posh-lookin. It was them put it all up in the first place, the cross and all the rest. Two of them I recognized. They took pictures with their phones. Opened some cans and poured them out on the ground.

ADAM: Grammar boys. Love their liturgical moment. There's training for you.

JUNE: But they never came back.

ADAM: Never?

JUNE: And you keep . . . I was comin to ask,
    actually to tell you.

ADAM: Ah, peace be with you, boys. [*he makes the
    sign of the cross in ironic blessing*] And also with
    you.

JUNE: Please. Stop.

ADAM: What a fucking joke.

JUNE: Stop that. Stop knockin everthin down!
    I want you to stop it!

ADAM: What? You? You're telling me?

JUNE: Askin?

ADAM: June, love. A boy's life. A woman's only
    child, a man's son.

JUNE: It's a sacred place.

ADAM: That squalid little shrine? A roadside cliché,
    that's what it is. A sentimental white cross – you
    think that's sufficient to the sacred memory of
    my son? And all the other dross hanging off it
    like birdshit – you think some spilled bourbon

and a few moronic slogans speak for Jack and who he was? JACK LIVES HERE, you reckon that does him justice? YOU CAN GET IT FLYING, YOU CAN GET IT DYIN . . . MATTER OF FACT I GOT IT NOW. Or how about STAY A LITTLE LONGER, that's a goodie. Eh? Eh? You know, his mother and I, June, we wouldn't have minded if Jack'd stayed a little longer. See him grown up, married maybe, kids. Yes, some things are sacred, dearie, but they're sacred to *us*, to the people who loved him.

JUNE *exits in tears.* ADAM *subsides into his chair, into memory and grief. For a moment he sings drunkenly.*

ADAM: And your mommy won't mind . . . And your daddy won't mind . . .

Light fades as the refrain from 'Stay (Just a Little Bit Longer)' takes ADAM *into memory.*

SCENE 7

Darkness. An insistent knock at the door. ADAM *lies adrift in his chair.*

MARY: [*off*] Don't get up. Don't get it.

ADAM: But Mary.

The knocking persists.

MARY: [*off*] No. Please! Don't ever get it.

ADAM: Love?

MARY: If we don't answer the door it'll never happen. It'll just pass by.

ADAM: But it keeps knocking.

MARY: Always.

ADAM: In my head.

MARY: In my heart.

ADAM: It'll always be knocking.

Lights up on MARY *at stage right. She stands with her phone in a cold island of light.* ADAM *gropes for his phone, startled.*

ADAM: June?

MARY: You're asleep again. I can't believe you can sleep, as if the world is alright. Who's June?

ADAM: What?

MARY: Who is she? Tell me.

ADAM: I tried to.

MARY: You never say a thing.

ADAM: It's her. This business at the . . . scene, the roadside.

MARY: I've told you, I don't want to know about that.

ADAM: You see?

MARY: I don't want to see it.

ADAM: I know.

MARY: What does she look like?

ADAM: What possible difference could it make
what she looks like? She's a Fenton.

MARY: All these months there's a girl.

ADAM: No. Well, yes.

MARY: In town.

ADAM: Well, she turned up. At the house.

MARY: This total stranger, this creature, you're
talking to her?

ADAM: Well—

MARY: You bastard.

ADAM: Don't be jealous.

MARY: Of course I'm jealous.

ADAM: Christ, she's a Fenton.

MARY: Not just her. I'm jealous that you're sleeping.

ADAM: That's not sleep, love, that's anaesthesia.
Christ, I'm drinking the cellar just to get over the
edge.

MARY: And you're talking to a stranger. Some girl.

ADAM: I'll tell you everything.

MARY: Don't. You won't. I know you won't.

ADAM: I will. I'll call you. Maybe I'll write it down.
Just settle down, love—

MARY: I'll never settle down.

ADAM: You just need some rest, love. Sleep.

MARY: Sleep, he says, take the pills. But I can't
sleep.

ADAM: Please.

MARY *hangs up.*

MARY: This is what happens when you break the
rules. A woman's not supposed to invest so much.

But I don't care about the shop, don't want to
finish the bloody MA. I am his mother.

ADAM: This is why they say don't have them.
I used to think that was sad, selfish. But that's
why people don't have kids.

MARY: Because of the fear.

ADAM: Because you're either afraid of them or
afraid for them.

MARY: Scared of this apocalypse, this annihilation.

ADAM: And when they're gone the hole they leave is
bigger than the space they took. How can that be?

MARY: I wish I'd listened. I'd still be myself.
Childless, coherent, consistent, strong.

Light up on JACK *upstage.* MARY *flips the phone open again
and dials.*

JACK: You know the drill. Leave a message. Love
you, Mum. I know it's you. You can't keep doing
this. Still love ya.

A long, eerie beep. And JUNE *is there at the roadside shrine.
She strokes the burn scars on her belly, struggling to retain
control.*

JUNE: It's orright, you're orright. See? June, you're
orright. You have to. You owe it to him. Just tell
him, you stupid, ugly, fat bitch!

Jack (Paul Ashcroft) and June (Whitney Richards)

SCENE 8

At the roadside two teenage boys in suits stand by the wounded tree and the shrine in dappled light. WILL *has a sticking plaster on his forehead.* BEN's *arm is in a sling. They pour out booze upon the earth at the foot of the cross. As if at the sound of an inquisitorial voice they turn to speak.*

WILL: Jack was at the wheel.

BEN: Yeah, yes, it was Jack driving. Sir.

Light on ADAM *as their* LAWYER. *He stands in his livingroom like a barrister in chambers, his manner at once inquisitorial and conspiratorial.*

ADAM/LAWYER: And yet the Mansfield boy, his body was found outside the vehicle.

WILL: No seatbelt?

ADAM/LAWYER: And, of course, the car in three pieces.

WILL: Right.

BEN: Just shit – like, sorry, stuff.

WILL: Everywhere.

BEN: Clothes.

WILL: Door.

BEN: Boards.

WILL: In bits.

BEN: Bits.

WILL: And it was raining. And quiet. For a long time it was quiet.

BEN: Birds. I could hear the wind in the trees.

ADAM/LAWYER: Were you conscious when the first vehicle arrived?

BEN: Think so.

WILL: I dunno. Don't remember. But I remember the lights.

BEN: The ambulance. The fireys.

WILL: Yes, I remember the fireys.

ADAM/LAWYER: As they cut you free?

BEN: Right.

ADAM/LAWYER: Yet it was several minutes before they found young Jack?

WILL: I don't know anything, we don't know anything about that.

ADAM/LAWYER: It's in the record. That you, Will, that you told the paramedic Jack had already left the scene, that he'd gone for help or just run off.

WILL: No. I don't remember saying it. Maybe I did. I was pretty—

ADAM/LAWYER: Concussed, yes it's there in the record. Did you hear him say this, Ben? Did you hear Will say this?

BEN: Um. I don't, I don't recall?

Light on MARY *at a distance.*

MARY: He always wore a seatbelt. You little shits.

ADAM/LAWYER: Remind me again, son. What're you studying?

BEN: Geology. Sir.

ADAM/LAWYER: And you, Will?

WILL: Well. [*shrugs*] Law. Sir.

ADAM/LAWYER: [*pondering this*] Your father, Ben?

BEN: He's flying back from China.

ADAM/LAWYER: And Will, I spoke to your dad this morning.

WILL: The office?

ADAM/LAWYER: No, we both swim at North Cott every morning.

WILL: You've got the corporate box, then. Eagles.

ADAM/LAWYER: Hmm. Now, had you boys been drinking?

BEN: Um.

WILL: Yeah. Yes. All night.

BEN: Fair bit. That's why.

WILL: Like why—

ADAM/LAWYER: Why this other boy was driving. Because neither of you was in a fit state.

WILL: Yeah, that's it.

ADAM/LAWYER: And how fast were you going?

BEN: Don't remember.

ADAM/LAWYER: You were . . . what, passed out?

WILL: Yeah, that's it.

ADAM/LAWYER: In the back, in the rear seat of the vehicle? With your seatbelt on?

WILL *nods carefully.*

ADAM/LAWYER: At 7.45. In the morning.

BEN: I feel bad. That we, you know, left him to drive. Like, I feel a bit, you know, responsible?

319

WILL: Like, we coulda told him to slow down?

ADAM/LAWYER: If you hadn't been asleep in the
back.

WILL: [*cottoning on*] Yeah.

BEN: He was a good bloke, but.

ADAM/LAWYER: Jack Mansfield?

As if summoned, JACK *appears at the forest edge.*

WILL: Yeah. We'll . . . he'll, you know, he'll be
missed. He'll be sadly missed by all and sundry.

MARY: Christ! I've heard politicians sound more
sincere. You're already suing us, you scum!

ADAM: [*as himself*] It's just the insurance company,
love, it's not personal.

MARY: He's not even cold and you want
recompense for your injuries? Your interrupted
pre-season? Your inability to drive yourself to
uni, to lift a pint at Steve's? When you left him
out there in the rain so long he was beyond
saving? You lying shitheads!

The boys flinch and wince.

ADAM: Mary, it's only money. And it's not even our money; it's insurance.

MARY: It's the principle.

ADAM: Just a process.

MARY: Like grief, you mean? How do you let an outrage become a process? What species of domestication is this? Only a man could call a bushfire a process. Stand in your burning house and tell me that, why don't you!

The boys break themselves free from proceedings and begin their exit.

BEN: Fuck.

WILL: Women.

BEN: Why'd you tell 'em?

WILL: Fuck, man. Wouldn't've made any difference. It was like fifteen minutes before anyone showed. He was rooted.

BEN: But why'd you say it?

WILL: I didn't. I don't remember saying it.

BEN: Bullshit.

WILL: Don't be a pussy.

WILL *exits, pulling out his phone.* BEN *stares into the gloom of the forest as if into the fresh grave itself. He is haunted by his guilt, his collusion. The entire adult world of privilege and patronage has become clear to him. And amidst the shadows* JACK MANSFIELD *stands pale and silent.*

Adam/Lawyer (John Howard), Will (Luke McMahon) and Ben (Will McNeill)

SCENE 9

ADAM's *beach house at dusk next evening. He stares out the window, already a little drunk, a glass of wine in one hand and a pair of binoculars in the other.*

> ADAM: Dolphins! Three, four, five, six of them. Winding round the Point in the last, faint light, backs shining, all surfing the same wave, just – yes! – bursting from the water like . . . like an actual moment of grace. And then suddenly gone. Mary, love, you should have seen it. [*abruptly angry*] You should have let yourself see it. Why the hell don't you ever come down? He loved it here.

Light on JUNE *at the door. Her appearance is sudden enough to startle him. He spills wine, sets both glass and binoculars aside and tries to wipe himself down haplessly.* JUNE *bears a carton of groceries. She offers it and he accepts it clumsily.*

JUNE: I work two days at the IGA. Expired stuff.
   I thought maybe . . .

ADAM: Oh. Great. That's . . . that's a lot of Sui
   Min noodles. And look, asparagus, from—

JUNE: Peru.

ADAM: Peru.

JUNE: Makes your wee stink.

ADAM: What?

JUNE: Makes it smell like twenty-year-old semillon.

ADAM: Semillon?

JUNE: Sorry. That was kinda . . .

ADAM: What makes your wee stink like semillon?

JUNE: Asparagus.

ADAM: Just the stuff from Peru?

JUNE: No, all of it. I thought you'd know.

ADAM: Well. Consider me freshly enlightened. How d'you know what an old semillon smells like, anyway?

JUNE: Well.

ADAM: I'm curious. You don't mind me being a bit curious, do you?

JUNE: I'm exaggeratin. About the wine, not the wee.

ADAM: Sniff a lot of urine, do you?

JUNE: What?

ADAM: Seriously, I'm curious. About how you know what such an unfashionable wine smells like.

JUNE: I'm a cellarhand, remember?

ADAM: But we've never done a straight semillon.

JUNE: Oh. That's right.

ADAM: And nothing twenty years old.

JUNE: No. Doesn't really smell like that, anyway. I dunno why I said it.

ADAM: Thought you didn't drink wine.

JUNE: No. Not now.

ADAM: So, the old semillons, where'd you come across them?

JUNE: Um? Jack? Jack showed me.

ADAM: Jack? My Jack?

JUNE: He was tryin to explain.

ADAM: But he didn't know anything about wine.

JUNE: Oh, nah, he knew a lot. Truly. And downstairs there's heaps.

ADAM: You've been in my cellar?

JUNE: He showed me the old Peter Lehmanns and the Tyrell's. A couple from Margaret River. One from Balingup. So different.

ADAM: What d'you mean, he showed you?

JUNE: Well, he opened them all and we tasted 'em. Sorry. I mean we didn't drink the lot, we just spat, mostly. Maybe that's worse, eh?

ADAM: [*still holding the box*] I didn't realize.

JUNE: [*warming to the task, feeding his excitement*]
You gotta love the Hunter Valley stuff. The old
Elizabeths. The Lovedales. Labels all curled off.
All gold in the glass.

ADAM: Exactly. Gorgeous.

JUNE: That pineappley, burnt-toasty kinda—

ADAM: The ugly duckling of Australian wine, June.
You can't give them away.

JUNE: But that's what's special. It's beautiful and no
one sees it. Jack saw it. He knew.

ADAM: But he never showed the slightest interest.
I didn't know.

JUNE: Hell, you should have seen him with the
Lindeman's.

ADAM: The bloody Lindeman's! They were stashed,
buried. How'd he even find 'em? He must've
been reading my notes.

JUNE: [*carefully*] Maybe.

ADAM: The cunning little . . . God, does he even

know what those museum releases are worth?

JUNE: Well, you might want to think about the '74. It's kind of tanking. I'd drink it now or sell 'em.

ADAM: Jesus, why not rip the scab off the '71 while you're at it?

JUNE: [*wincing guiltily*] Oops.

ADAM: Why didn't he tell me? Why couldn't he do that with me?

JUNE: I don't know.

ADAM: What was it like, the '71?

JUNE: Like him. Like Jack. Had a kind of . . . I don't know . . . afterglow? Is that the right word?

ADAM *is consumed by this news, the image. He almost forgets she's there and takes a few moments to catch himself.*

ADAM: Geez. You've got a real nose, June.

JUNE: Yeah. That's what they said at school.

ADAM: I meant in the olfactory sense.

JUNE: Me mum couldn't smell a thing.

ADAM: Some people aren't gifted.

JUNE: It wasn't that. Dad bashed her.

ADAM: Ah. Well, here, make yourself at home. Obviously you know your way round. I did notice a few gaps in the cellar. Thought it was me. I seem to have developed quite a thirst.

JUNE: Well. No one could blame you. The time you've had.

ADAM: Ah, I was hitting it pretty hard, even before.

JUNE: I know the feelin.

ADAM *looks at her, puzzling over some detail in her story, not completely convinced but wanting so badly to believe her.*

ADAM: You really knew him, then.

JUNE: Yeah.

ADAM: Things I didn't even know.

JUNE: You're surprised.

ADAM: Well, yes.

JUNE: That someone like me could know him.

ADAM: Well, no, not in those terms. Obviously he'd come down all those years for his holidays and to pick, and then, later with his mates when they'd come surfing. Of course you'd know *of* him. It's a small place. But I just didn't think you'd know him well enough to—

JUNE: To be here. In your house, your cellar.

ADAM: What can I get you to drink?

JUNE: Just water.

ADAM: Just water? Just water.

JUNE *sees the binoculars. Emboldened, she takes them up to scan the paddock and the sea. Before he brings her glass,* ADAM *observes her. He can't help but survey her with a man's practised and habitual eye.*

ADAM: Course I'm surprised. Who wouldn't be? This sad, lumpy girl in her tufty jumper and Blundstones. I mean, if she really had something you'd understand. Every little town's got its flawed jewel, the girl who's close enough to beautiful. But June Fenton?

He takes the glass of water to her.

ADAM: So, you like the surf. The surfers.

JUNE *lowers the binoculars and stares at him reproachfully.*
ADAM *does his best to recover.*

> ADAM: I mean, I'm the same. I could watch them
> all day. Always regret I never did it as a young
> man.

> JUNE: Because the girls liked it?

> ADAM: No, no. Just . . . the freedom. Don't spose
> you surf yourself?

> JUNE: Hardly. Fell in one day when I was a
> kid, when they were openin the rivermouth.
> Remember gettin sucked along and all these
> snapper bumpin into me on their way to the sea.
> Someone pulled me out with a gaff. Catch of the
> day. Bag of rubbish. Nah, I just watch.

> ADAM: Me too. I envy them. Some days it's all I do.

> JUNE: And you read, I see. Stories?

> ADAM: Stories? No, what's the point?

> JUNE: So you read, what, fact books?

> ADAM: I've got no patience for make-believe.

> JUNE: So what's this then?

ADAM: [*amused*] Well, here you've caught me
   out. This bloke's a biologist. Thinks nature has
   feelings. He's all about, and I quote: 'mentality
   existing in some form all the way down to
   quarks'.

JUNE: I don't know what that means.

ADAM: Well, June, that's two of us. I mean, what's
   his story, eh?

JUNE: [*blankly*] I spose it passes the time.

ADAM: No. [*he drinks off his wine*] Time passes
   anyway. It doesn't require any help from us.

JUNE: You're angry.

He stares at her appraisingly.

JUNE: It's none of my business.

ADAM: But you said it anyway.

JUNE: It's normal. Being angry. When someone
   dies.

ADAM: Jesus, June. Spare me the self-help section,
   will you?

JUNE: Sorry.

ADAM: No, I'm the one who should be saying sorry.

He pours himself another drink.

ADAM: Yes, I am angry. But it's nothing to be afraid of. It'll pass in a minute.

JUNE: But it doesn't, does it. I've seen you. Out on the bend at the shrine.

ADAM: I told you. That's different. That's not how I want him remembered.

JUNE: With alcohol, you mean?

ADAM: What?

JUNE: Or is it just beer and bourbon you don't approve of?

ADAM: It's ugly, shallow, coarse.

JUNE: But his mates put it up.

ADAM: Well, he wasn't their son and they weren't his mates.

JUNE: I know.

ADAM: You wouldn't have a clue.

JUNE: Orright.

ADAM: No, June, I won't have it.

JUNE: It's better than nothin. Better than not
     rememberin him at all.

ADAM: It's not where he lived, it's not how he lived,
     it's just where he died.

JUNE: And you come down anyway. More and
     more. With no real reason, 'cause you're out of the
     wine business. You drive by all the time. You slow
     down, you get out. You stand there for hours.

ADAM: I stop and get out because of that travesty.
     Because of what those cowards, those suckholes
     put up to make 'emselves look good, feel better.
     That's why I'm angry.

JUNE: Nah. You're angry at *him*.

ADAM: Oh June. Very clever.

JUNE: For a local yokel, you mean.

ADAM: For a person of your tender age.

JUNE: [*bitterly*] Tender age.

ADAM: You're young, that's all.

JUNE: In court once. In front of everyone. The lawyer said I was, and I quote: 'wise beyond my years as a result of things witnessed at a tender age'. All my life I wanted to forget those words. But you see I learnt them by heart.

ADAM: Well, you've made a silk purse out of a sow's ear.

JUNE: You make it sound disgustin.

ADAM: Well, I am disgusted. But not at you.

JUNE: Whatever.

ADAM: It's just that he had so much more. He had everything, love. A safe, happy home, all the advantages, every privilege. And he's wasted himself.

JUNE: It wasn't really his fault.

ADAM: It's killed us, me and his mother. I mean, what's his legacy, what's he left us? Pain that'll never go away. We're nearly finished. As a couple, as functioning people, because he didn't have the guts to stand up to the Hooray Henries he ran with.

JUNE: No. That's not right.

ADAM: No consolation, nothing noble to cling to. What do we have, June, but a wasteful death, another indulged, meaningless schoolboy road death? The usual empty phrases, the awkward posturing. 'Cut down in the prime of his life. Happy-go-lucky. Would've done anything for ya. Top bloke.' It's pitiful, shameful. It's actually embarrassing.

JUNE: You're embarrassed?

ADAM: Yes, and ashamed for feeling it.

JUNE: It's the country. People die in cars. They die on the toilet. You can't judge someone by his death.

ADAM: Well, you do. If you're honest you do.

JUNE: He had an accident. He was barely nineteen. He didn't get time for a Nobel Prize. What do you want?

ADAM: I want him back, you hear me? I want him back!

Blackout. Sound of the thundering ocean.

SCENE 10

Sound of the roaring sea. Enter BEN *and* WILL *in wetsuits, carrying their boards up the beach after a surf.*

WILL: Fuckin tide. Gone all fat'n mushy.

BEN: God, it's hell cold.

They toss down their boards and gaze back out to sea as they unzip their wetsuits and begin peeling them off. As they speak, BEN *dresses beneath the screen of his towel.* WILL *is far less shy.*

WILL: Look at him, willya. First in, last out.

But BEN *has noticed something else, someone else approaching along the beach.*

WILL: What?

BEN: That chick again.

WILL: The bushpig.

BEN: Fuck, man, she's like a stalker.

WILL: Ugly bitch.

BEN: [*laughs*] Shut up, she'll hear ya.

WILL: Like I care.

Enter JUNE *who gazes out to sea.*

WILL: [*to* BEN] Well, mate, you were shit out there
   today.

BEN: Fuck off. Head's still spinnin from last night.

WILL: Shiraz poisoning, you gay prick.

BEN: Can you believe how much piss there is in
   that house?

WILL: Didn't even make a dent in it. Like three
   dark walls of tannins and histamines and . . .
   I dunno what the fuck I'm talkin about.

BEN: Reckon I like Bundy better anyway. Dja bring
   it?

WILL: Mate, you're on a mission this week.

BEN: Why not? Only young'n beautiful once.

WILL: Look at these locals. Fuckin kooks.

JUNE: Whenever the swell's up, half the tradies in
town are in the water. Wetsuits shiny as seals.
Locals, mostly. And some blow-ins like Jack.
Wood-ducks, we call 'em. Fly in, shit all over the
joint and flap away again. But Jack always stood
out; I remember him all the way back when I was
still in school. I watched him for years. But that
makes it sound kind of weird. It wasn't. There
was nothin wrong about it.

Enter JACK, *beachcombing below.*

JUNE: Seemed lonely to me. Different. I mean,
apart from that creamy-smooth look those
private-school city boys have. Used to walk
the beach, pick stuff up – coloured glass, sand
dollars. He had a thong collection.

JACK: [*stooping*] Yeah!

*He brandishes a sunbleached thong, examines it like a
connoisseur.*

JUNE: Must've had hundreds of 'em. Specially after

339

I noticed. Cause I used to go down at night, or
sometimes early in the mornin and plant 'em.
Thongs. Yeah. When I started at the IGA it's
what I spent half me money on. Used to bleach
'em and bake 'em, drop battery acid on 'em.
Make 'em look all weathered and beaten up,
like they'd floated from Brazil or Africa. God, he
loved my thongs. And I never told him. He saved
me. But I never got to tell him. That all those
years he thought the sea was bringin in those odd
thongs, it was really just me. Just the local girl.
The bushpig. Stickin 'em out there for him to
find.

JACK *wanders off, beaming, with his find.* JUNE *follows a little
way as the light fades towards dusk.*

> JUNE: He had no idea who I was. Years. Not even
> on the beach that last day.

> WILL: Inbred deviants.

> JUNE: Okay, maybe I was a bit obsessive.

> BEN: Show us ya harelip, mate!

> JUNE: But isn't that just, like . . . love? Doesn't it
> need somethin unreasonable, somethin wild to
> break free and fly?

BEN *and* WILL *indulge in a bit of horseplay upstage. They turn and watch as a surfer takes off out in the break and then they wince and roar as he takes a nasty wipeout.*

WILL: Here we go, local genius.

BEN: Come on, son, use your arms.

WILL: Like ya mean it, ya gumby.

BEN: Uh-oh.

WILL: Ugly.

BEN: Sinus-flush.

WILL: Suck it up, son!

JUNE: I was a ghost out there at the Point. Like I was invisible. Until that Friday.

BEN: End of first semester.

WILL: And raining.

BEN: Well, it's south, right? It's winter.

JUNE: It was cold, drizzly. The rivermouth was open. The sea was the colour of stewed tea.

JACK *enters in his wetsuit with a surfboard. He sets the board down and struggles to get hold of the zip over his shoulder, ends up turning like a dog patiently following its tail.* JUNE *laughs and* JACK *sees that he's being watched. As he finally gets hold of the tag, he waves in sheepish acknowledgement.*

JUNE: You look blue.

JACK: Nah, I'm quite cheerful, actually. Can't feel me fingers, but.

JUNE: Your lips.

JACK: Lips?

JUNE: Your lips're blue.

JACK: Ah. That's kind of . . . embarrassing.

They maintain an awkward silence and JUNE *pulls her hood up and shoves her hands into her pockets, hunching against the weather.* ADAM *emerges behind her, observing.*

JACK: Hey, you wanna get warm?

JACK *squats and lights a driftwood fire.* JUNE *shrugs, hesitates, and then before she joins him she addresses* ADAM *who stands by the window, still listening to her story.* WILL *and* BEN *join* JACK *at the fire.*

JUNE: And I guess that's how I got to spend a day
with Jack. And those two.

She sits by the fire close to JACK.

JUNE: It rained all afternoon. Waves piling into the
bay. All the peppy scrub drippin. The granite
headland grey and streaked with runoff. And
the light started to bleed away, like . . . like the
minutes leakin from the day, and the weaker it
got, the more wired I felt. Like . . . mad. Too
excited.

BEN *and* JACK *pour rum into a litre bottle of cola while* WILL
*packs a juice-bottle bong with dope. Bottle and bong are passed
around.*

BEN: Bundyburger with the lot!

WILL: Rumdiddlyumptious!

JUNE: Other people just drifted away, and there was
no one about in the end except us. Four of us.
The fire. Rum. A bong. And him right there. It
got dark.

BEN: [*to* JUNE] Get that into ya.

WILL: Yeah, suck on that.

BEN: Jack's friend.

WILL: Jack's shadow.

JUNE: June.

JUNE *drags on the bong as the boys laugh, and then she takes a long chug from the bottle.*

BEN: June.

WILL: June, June, loves her goon.

ADAM: And what'd you talk about? You and Jack.

JUNE: [*a little vague and giggly*] Nothin. Talked shit, really. With them there, it was . . . well, we were just gettin bombed.

ADAM: What did he say? My son. What was he saying?

JUNE: He was shy. It was kind of agonizin – *they* did all the talkin. I was just happy. Sittin next to him. Jack. By the fire. Up close. Breeze pourin in off the sea. His knee against mine. Mine. Don't you remember what that was like?

ADAM: Yes.

JUNE: He smelt of coconut. And that clean sea
    smell. And all smoky from the fire. And we're
    chuggin and smokin mull and the sea's roarin in
    me ears and . . . I was so happy I thought I'd die.
    And then the fire's spinnin, the sand's kind of
    pulsin. Everythin rushin up inside me like —

ADAM: Love? Hope?

JUNE: No, I puked.

The boys roar and recoil.

WILL: She's chirped!

BEN: Chick. Chirp.

JACK: Yeah, I get it.

JUNE: I staggered out onto the beach. So . . .
    just . . . totally wasted. And I've yacked all down
    me jumper.

*JUNE hauls off her pullover and moves to stage front to stoop to
wash the garment at the shore.*

BEN: Look out, you inebriate!

WILL: Invertebrate!

345

A roar from the boys as a wave knocks JUNE *aside. She staggers, falls, spluttering. On all fours, she tries to get to her feet.* JACK *gets up from his spot at the fire, snatches up a towel and goes unhurriedly to help.*

JACK: Fuck, man, she's a mess. Gimme a hand.

WILL: Piss off, I'm all dry and warm now.

BEN: You go, mate, we'll shepherd.

JACK: Wankers.

WILL: Well, she's *your* shadow, mate.

BEN: Secret admirer.

WILL: Better when they're house-trained.

JACK *goes down to* JUNE. *Hesitates. Tries to get hold of her without touching anything important.* JUNE *crawls, writhes, rolls.*

WILL: Aw, look what he's found washed up.

BEN: Flotsam, mate.

WILL: Jetsam, actually.

BEN: Same diff.

JACK *gets* JUNE *to her feet. Their gaze meets for a moment. He looks back towards the others.* JUNE *looks back as well. They are transfixed. The sea rumbles around them. Wild laughter from* BEN *and* WILL. *Pounding surf.*

JACK: I should take her home.

JUNE: It was hardly anythin.

BEN: Nothing!

WILL: It's just bullshit.

JACK: Should walk her up the track to the house.

JUNE: Nothin really happened.

JACK: I'm too pissed to drive.

ADAM: What did he do? Jack!

BEN: Nothing!

JUNE: Nothin I could've said.

WILL: No one there to see.

JUNE: Nothin that felt clear enough, you know, straightforward enough to say in front of strangers. Like, officially.

JACK: She's cold.

JUNE: Soaked. Everythin. It was freezin, the wind, the shirt.

JACK: Just a girl. Cold, staggering. On her own.

JUNE: Freezin.

JACK: The fire.

JUNE: Fire.

JACK: Here by the fire.

Still leaning on JACK's *arm,* JUNE *unbuttons her sopping shirt. He turns away politely, pushes the towel her way. She shrugs out of her shirt and wraps herself in the towel, still wearing her bra.* JACK *leads her back to the flickering light of the fire.*

JUNE: Just. I think I pulled it off. The wet stuff, the jumper, the shirt. And the fire was warm.

At the fireside JACK *gives* JUNE *a beanie and as she reaches to pull it on the towel falls open.*

BEN: Fuck! Look out!

WILL: Man, that's full-on.

ADAM *peers down.* BEN *and* WILL *begin to poke and paw at her belly.*

JACK: What is it?

ADAM: June, what is that?

For a moment JUNE *submits woozily to their examination.*

JUNE: [*to* ADAM] I wasn't thinkin. I shouldn't have taken off the shirt. I'd already forgotten the others were there.

ADAM: What is this? What're those marks?

JUNE: When I was thirteen, fourteen. Used to sit by the wood stove at night. Mum'd drink herself to sleep hopin the old man wouldn't come home. And once she passed out I used to get a knittin needle. Stick it in the fire. Just keep meself awake. Keep meself to meself.

ADAM: They look like—

JUNE: [*bitterly*] Yeah, like stretchmarks. Knittin needle. She said she wished she'd used it when she had the chance. Wouldn't have to put up with the likes of me.

WILL: Fuck, that's messed up.

ADAM: How long did you do this to yourself?

JUNE: Wanted to say what happened. Try.

ADAM: Happened?

WILL: Sick little piggy.

BEN: She's gunna fall in the fire.

JACK: What're you doing?

WILL: Doing?

BEN: Nothing.

JUNE: I'm fallin.

JACK: Shivering.

WILL: Just lying there.

JUNE: Well. Actually. Somethin did happen.

JUNE *sags a moment and is held up by* BEN *and* WILL. *They lie her down by the fire. Their predatory faces are lit by firelight.* JACK *hesitates, anxious, uncertain.*

JACK: It was like . . . like the temperature suddenly
    drops. Her skin's sandy, and there are bubbles of

foam on her belly. And in the firelight, fine hairs
like on a peach. But those marks. Scars. Like
she'd pulled herself through barbed wire. Not
once. But again and again. And then the others.

BEN: Giss a look.

WILL: Fuck, man.

BEN: Fuck.

JACK: You could feel it, the suck of breath.
    Everyone's heart rate leaping. It was like a shot
    of something.

JUNE: Numb. I was numb.

JACK: Damage, that's what it was.

JUNE: Too numb to feel it comin.

JACK: The sight of damage. Like it did something
    to them. Us.

WILL: Nothing.

JACK: To us, maybe. I thought: They're only
    warmin her up, they're only muckin around. But
    they had their hands on her.

JUNE: [*woozy*] What? Everythin turnin, turnin.

BEN: Cool. She's got stripes.

JUNE: Like I'm still tumblin in the water. These things, these creatures, bumpin, slidin, nippin at me. Tentacles, mouths.

WILL: Did you do it anywhere else?

BEN: Giss a look.

WILL: Here, let's slip this off. Oh, looky here.

JUNE: [*woozy, obscured*] What? What're you doin?

JACK: Firelight. Hands everywhere. She was wet, shivering.

JUNE: And it's like I'm lookin up through water.

WILL: Aw, yeah.

JUNE: Lookin for a face. I can't find his face.

JACK: Got dark. Even in my heart it got dark.

JUNE: No.

BEN: I smell bushpig.

WILL: Mm-mm! Country bacon. Tasty.

JUNE: No. Stop.

JACK: Stop it. What're you doing?

JUNE: And suddenly he's there. All wavy and watery in the firelight.

JACK: And I'm standing there, doing nothing. And they're . . . like she's a thing.

WILL: Fuck, where's the camera, get ya phone, mate.

BEN: Nah, I don't reckon we should.

JACK: Stop it. I should have said it. Done something. But she did it for me.

JUNE: He stopped it. He saved me.

JACK: I just bloody stood there.

JUNE: No! Get off.

WILL: [obscured] Ow! Fuckin bit me!

JACK: And suddenly she's up.

BEN: Running.

JACK: Right past me.

JUNE: Runnin.

JACK: Out into the dark.

JUNE: The noise, the rain, the night.

JACK: With no one.

JUNE: Just runnin.

ADAM: Jesus Christ.

Blackout.

From left: Adam (John Howard), Ben (Will McNeill),
June (Whitney Richards) and Will (Luke McMahon)

SCENE 11

Lights up on JUNE *at stage right, dishevelled and shivering at the shore.* ADAM *watches from his beach house.*

> JUNE: No wind at all. Don't know why I remember. But it stopped. Still cold, but the wind had just . . . like the world holdin its breath. I was out of my mind.

> ADAM: You were drunk, June. Stoned.

> JUNE: I ran into the water. Right up there against the Point, close to the rocks. Could feel the rip suckin at my legs. I was so hot. My skin felt scorched. And the water was so clean and cold. It was good to feel clean. Even if it hurt.

Light on JACK *upstage.*

JACK: Just a white flash. That's all I saw.

Light on WILL *and* BEN *on the beach at stage left. Both have a bottle of wine in hand.*

WILL: Stupid bitch. I'll need a rabies shot.

BEN: Maybe we shouldna.

WILL: What?

BEN: Well. Feels weird. I feel crook.

WILL: Pussy.

BEN: Should make sure – maybe.

WILL: I'm outta here. What're you waitin for? True
    love?

BEN: The fuck is he?

WILL: Telling her all about his social conscience.
    His trip to Cambodia.

BEN: I didn't know he'd been to Cambodia.

WILL: He hasn't.

BEN: So, what about Cambodia?

WILL: Fuck, man, you must've slept the whole way down. All he ever talks about.

BEN: What's this one? Grenache. Man, where's Grenache?

WILL: Ask him when he gets in.

BEN: Man, he doesn't know shit about wine. Told me himself.

WILL: What, when you were learning all about digging wells in Cambodia? Where the fuck is he?

BEN: She got in the water.

WILL: Didn't see.

BEN: Yeah, full noise, straight in, like it was nothing. Like it was a warm bath she was heading for.

WILL: Like I said, I never saw. Dark. Didn't see a thing, constable.

BEN: Fuck. Right. And she's probably just tryna get his attention.

WILL: Creeps me out, that chick. There's somethin

wrong with her.

BEN: Still. Hope she didn't do anything stupid. I mean we're just mucking around.

WILL: I don't recall.

BEN: What?

WILL: My memory's unclear.

BEN: Oh. Right. [*considers this collusion*]

WILL: That's all I know, constable. [*peers at the bottle in hand*] Constable Cabernet Sauvignon. New, are ya? From what, France, are ya? I don't care what kind of fancypants detective y'are with ya beret and ya—

BEN: Cause it was dark.

WILL: And she was pissed. A lot of alcohol was involved.

BEN: And if anyone got with her it was—

WILL: Flash Jack Mansfield.

BEN: But we didn't see it.

WILL: We were up at the house, playin—

BEN: Monopoly.

WILL: Scrabble.

BEN: Nah, it was Monopoly.

WILL: Have it your way, Sherlock. Let's get
hammered.

BEN *and* WILL *collect their stuff and exit.*

JUNE: It was like being too close to the fire. Being
sucked in. The cold as hot as the fire, hot as my
skin. The rip, like the river. Smooth rocks goin
by. And I'm awake again, properly awake. Happy.

ADAM: Happy? What're you talking about? You're
being dragged out to sea.

JUNE: Maybe not happy. Just resigned. Like this
was what I was always comin to, to be dragged
out like the trash built up in the inlet, somethin
best got rid of. Out past the Point it was calm.
No rocks, no trees. After a while I could see stars.
And when I moved there was a kind of twinkly
trail.

ADAM: Phosphorescence.

JUNE: Beautiful. Sparkles, creamy smears and swirls in the black. I thought: I don't know why I ever worried. Total dark. It's lovely. Like if this is it, I don't mind. I felt light, beautiful. For once I'm beautiful.

ADAM: June, you were in the ocean. Pissed. At night.

JUNE: But that's how I felt. I want to tell you, give somethin to you. Like a gift.

ADAM: While half in love with easeful death—

JUNE: What?

ADAM: June, those boys—

JUNE: Oh, forget 'em.

ADAM: Forget? How can I forget them?

JUNE: Some people are forgettable.

ADAM: I need to know. That is, can I ask you? Those boys, did they—

JUNE: Rape me?

ADAM: Christ—

JUNE: You could feel it. In the air. Breathe it, feel it comin. That's what they wanted, where it was goin, even if they didn't know.

ADAM: And Jack?

JUNE: No. I don't think so.

JACK: Nothing. I did bloody nothing.

JUNE: It's not clear. I dunno. I was—

ADAM: Asking for it?

JUNE: Out of it. It just took me too long to feel it comin, see it happenin. Way too long.

ADAM: And Jack? What did he do?

JUNE: Well.

ADAM: What, just sat there?

JACK: Stood. Stood there. Stupid as a bit of driftwood.

JUNE: It's murky. Like I was underwater.

ADAM: Tell me. No, don't tell me.

JUNE: It's orright, it's okay.

ADAM: How can it be?

JUNE: I'm tryin to give you somethin.

ADAM: What, a fright? Don't bother to call it a
wake-up 'cause I've had all the waking up I want in
a lifetime.

JUNE: I just want you to listen.

ADAM: Look, if he hurt you, if he did anything
untoward.

JUNE: No.

ADAM: Tell me the truth. No, don't tell me, I can't
bear it, I've got nothing left.

JUNE: He's frightened of hearin somethin worse.
How does it get any worse than what he thinks
of Jack? His own son. What do they all want,
these people with children? They all thinkin of
the knittin needle? That what they think?

ADAM: Look, June, I'm so sorry it happened.

JUNE: What's that, then?

ADAM: Whatever did happen.

JUNE: Just let me *tell* you. I felt him come.

ADAM: Oh, good God!

JUNE: Towards me. In the water. And then I could see.

JACK: What d'you do? I mean, I'm on the beach here, totally peakin. It's night and she's out there somewhere in the water, in the dark. Black as a dog's guts, truly, and there's these little white flashes. Something flickering, flashing. That's her, that'll be her out in the channel. So, I dunno what to do, what can I do? But finally I'm doing something. Running. I get me board and just paddle out, lookin for her. Swell's gone, no waves at all, just the rip goin out along the rocks. And I'm flying. I mean the current's really fast. When I paddle, every time me fingers go through the water, there's this creamy light, like milk coming off me fingertips. I mean, I'm a bit stoned, but I know this is real. And suddenly there's things moving out here, not just water, but bodies, water slapping against things I can't see. And, then, I'm way the hell out past the Point and the fire on the beach's gone and I can't see where I am anymore. There's this big, smooth rock sliding by and I'm thinking: Mate, there's no rocks out this far; you've got turned around in the dark, you're lost, this girl's gunna drown out here in the dark. She's cactus. And you've let it happen.

JUNE: The water gets cold, starts to smell bad. Now I'm shiverin. See these flashes, and I call out.

JACK: Jack!

JUNE: Jack!

JACK: That's what I hear, real close.

JUNE: And there's this—

Sound of a great, funnelling expiration. A deep, resonating moan.

JACK: Fuck!

JUNE: And starlight everywhere.

JACK: And there's a face.

JUNE: It's him. And I reach out and touch his hand.

JACK: And behind her—

JUNE: Behind him, this black hole.

JACK: With stars in it.

JUNE: Sequins, stars.

JACK: And I pull her on.

JUNE: And he's warm, like blood, and he doesn't even say anythin because he's lookin at somethin there in the dark, in the water, somethin so dark it's like all the nothin of your life gathered into one place, this incredible starry black—

JACK: Whale.

JUNE: That's right. A whale.

JACK: An arm's length away. Breathing on me.

JUNE: Two, three, four of 'em. All round us.

JACK: Just lying there.

JUNE: Breathin.

JACK: Breathing.

JUNE: Stinkin like . . . like anchovy breath. [*laughs*]

JACK: Are you alright?

JUNE: I can't believe it.

JACK: Are you alright?

JUNE: What? Yeah. Like I'm freezin me arse off
and I'm lost in the sea at night and I'm
surrounded by giant mammals. But, yeah, I'm
good – I think.

JACK: We stay here—

JUNE: Ages.

JACK: Forget what I'm supposed to be doing out
here, how far out we are, what the plan is.

JUNE: Shiny black skin. I can see stars reflected in it.

JACK: And that eye.

JUNE: Starlit, unblinkin eye.

JACK: And they're here, black as black, pressing like
memories.

JUNE: I feel different. I'm cold, yeah, but I can feel
them watchin. Like they see me. Really, I can
feel it all over. I dunno the right words for it,

the feel of being noticed, watched over. And this sighin and breathin and the buzz in the water goin right through me. It was Jack that afternoon, lookin up, when he finally saw me, made me real. That's how it is in the water, like I'm whole, like I exist. And I feel calm, safe. I'm happy.

JACK: I get hold of her, just hold on to her. We're both a bit hysterical by now, nearly gone. You know, hypothermic, floaty.

JUNE: Happy.

JACK: Half a mile out to sea. And she's holding me.

JUNE: He's holdin me.

JACK: Like she's safe already.

JUNE: On the beach, by the fire, with only him.

JACK *holds* JUNE *from behind. They are surrounded by stars.*

JACK: Like a dream we're having.

JUNE: No, it's real. I'm never this cold in a dream. It's never this black in a dream.

A torrential whoosh of whale breath.

JACK: Never smells this bad, either. Are you kicking?

JUNE: Of course I'm kickin. These boards aren't all that big, are they?

JACK: Feel that?

JUNE: Like an eddy.

JACK: They're turning. They know we're here. Even in the dark.

JUNE: They see us. I looked into an eye. Big, sad as an elephant's.

JACK: They're related, you know.

JUNE: Maybe they remember. Like elephants.

JACK: Maybe.

JUNE: That eye. Like a witness.

JACK: They use sonar. That's how they know we're here, that's how they keep track of each other, how they navigate. Echolocation.

JUNE: You mean they can feel us? In the dark?

JACK: I guess. Heartbeats, movement. Yeah.
I suppose the bigger, the darker your world,
the better you get at it.

JUNE: Look. Their skin looks like sky. Full of light,
of stars. We're kickin away in the dark. And he's
talkin, talkin all the time, like words are just
bubblin out of him. I love the sound of his voice.
There's no moon. The fire on the beach is out
already. The only light is the house on the hill. So
we aim for that. The whales let us through and for
a while we hear 'em behind us. And I just hold on
to the memory of 'em. I'm goin so numb and my
legs won't work. And I know if he just lets me go
he'd get in on his own and I start to feel like I'm
killin him, like if it wasn't for me he'd be fine, like
I'm just a load he has to carry. And I start to cry.
And he tries to stop me but I'm hopeless. Made
him promise he won't die.

JACK: June, I promise. No one's gonna die.

JUNE: He pushes me up onto the board and gets his
arms around me so I don't let go, and then tells
me to look at the light up on the hill and tells
me somethin he saw when he was a kid that he'd
never told anyone else in his life.

JACK: It's summer, a hot night. We're down for the
holidays, just the three of us, Mum and Dad

and me. You can smell the peppermints and
the sea and the straw smell of the vines pouring
down off the ridge in the breeze. I wake up and
go downstairs and they're both out there on the
deck at the rail. Mum's looking out to sea and
he's behind her. Lifting her skirt.

ADAM: Jesus!

JACK: It's so thin and fine you can see the ocean
through it, fizzing in the moonlight.

JUNE: And her legs were smooth and milky. And
there was this song on the stereo. And she was
holdin the rail. And you were—

ADAM: What's he doing telling you something like
that?

JUNE: And you pressed into her.

JACK: So . . . gently.

JUNE: And you were whisperin at her. He said it
was—

JACK: Beautiful. Like they are one thing, one
person.

JUNE: And he knew you loved each other and he

was yours. He knew it. He always knew it. I can
feel his chest against my back, his arms against
my arms. Whiskers at the back of my neck. I can
feel all of him, like I'm wearin him.

JACK: When I finally see it the beach is as white as a
summer bed.

JUNE: I think he carried me. Up the beach, the
track. It's messy in my head, this bit. We should
have yelled, celebrated, but we were too cold,
too tired. Soon as we were out of the water I
couldn't feel him, couldn't feel anythin. But
he got us to the house.

JACK: I help the girl upstairs.

JUNE: I think he pushes me into the shower. The
room is full of steam, like the inside of my head.
Feet just stumps. Can barely feel my hands. And
then the water starts to burn. God, it's like boilin
chip fat. I look around and there's no one in the
steam 'cept me, and it hurts.

JACK: I'm watching the kettle come to the boil.
She's still in the shower. I'm shaking, still in
me wetty. Ben and Will just lying there. And
I open the drawer, see the knives. That boning
knife. Their heads tossed back, throats right
there. I can feel the knife in my hand before

I reach for it. But then she starts crying. The
girl upstairs in the shower. Moaning. Like a cow.
My hands are shakin. I have to remember what
I'm there for. Milo. I'm there for Milo. I close
the knife drawer. I make her a hot drink. If she
hadn't made that noise I would have killed them.

JUNE: This arm comes in through the shower
   curtain and it's a mug and then I see Jack's face
   and he's totally white, just so scared, like I've
   really frightened him.

JACK: She pulls me in.

JUNE: And we stand under the water like that.
   Hours, it feels like. Just feelin ourselves come
   back. We got in bed, a big bed.

JACK *snuggles against* JUNE's *neck and slowly begins to sleep.*

JUNE: And he just held me like that all night.

ADAM: Well, that's probably enough detail on this
   subject.

JUNE: No, listen. I was embarrassed, really. Like, he
   must've been able to feel my big bum and see me
   ugly scars. I wondered if we'd get into it, if he'd
   want to—

ADAM: [*demurring*] June, really.

JUNE: And I didn't know if I'd want to. I think I
did want to, and now of course I wish.

Light on BEN *leaning in the doorway, drunk, hollow-eyed,
malevolent.*

JUNE: Except that Ben came in.

ADAM: What?

JUNE: I woke up and he was there in the doorway.

BEN: Came to in the kitchen. Felt crook.

JUNE: For a moment I thought he was a coat
hangin on the back of the door.

BEN: Like really crook. And I went to the bathroom
and there's water and clothes everywhere and a
wetty half out the door.

JUNE: And I guess that's what he's like anyway, Ben.

BEN: Followed all the water to the big room.

JUNE: He kind of hung there, starin.

BEN: Just wanted to see what happened. If he

was alright.

JUNE: Maybe if Will had been there he'd've filled up and become somethin – that's what I thought – maybe he'd do whatever it was he was thinkin about wantin to do. But he needed Will there to push him on.

BEN: And I guess I wanted to say something.

JUNE: Just starin.

ADAM: You woke him? You woke Jack?

JUNE: I don't even know if he was asleep. He was behind me. He didn't say anythin. I guess I felt safe. So I shut my eyes.

ADAM: And Ben's still there?

JUNE: No. He was suddenly—

BEN: Nothing.

JUNE: It was like, like . . . I closed my eyes and I'd killed him.

ADAM: They weren't his friends.

JUNE: I think he knew it. That weekend he saw it.

ADAM: I always saw it, right from the start. But it suited me. Their fathers, you see. Good school, good networks, good grounding. The Golden Triangle.

JUNE: I don't follow you.

ADAM: I wanted the best for him. You gotta do everything you can to maximize a kid's chances. You're parachuting them into hostile territory the moment they're born. You want him mixing with the right people, even if they're shits, because that's who they'll have to get on with if they want to crack a few nuts in the big smoke.

JUNE: It must be embarrassin, then. Findin out about him and me.

ADAM: Not at all. I'm glad of it.

JUNE: Now. Yeah, now you're glad. But a year or two ago you wouldna been, I bet.

ADAM: Well, a year or two ago I didn't know you.

JUNE: All you'd need to know is I'm a bushpig from the IGA. Just imagine. He falls in love. She's pregnant.

ADAM: But it didn't happen, Christ. You said

nothing happened.

JUNE: Everythin happened, everythin important
to me.

Jack (Paul Ashcroft) and June (Whitney Richards) in rehearsal

SCENE 12

The lawyer's office. BEN *and* WILL *sit in their new suits. There is no lawyer to hear them now. After a moment* JACK *appears behind them.* JUNE *lurks at a distance.*

JACK: At dawn she's gone. The girl.

BEN: Jack was spewin.

WILL: Angry as.

BEN: At us. For fuck's sake.

WILL: As if it's our fault she does a runner in the wee hours.

BEN: And that's the truth. That's why. He gets the chick into bed, something happens – or nothing happens, knowing him – and she takes off.

WILL: I mean, shit, she's from the country. She's expecting a bit of action.

BEN: But she's off.

WILL: Like *she* was something to brag about.

JUNE: It was just too much. Too much to take in. I should have stayed. But I was so embarrassed. I was a mess. And hurtin all over. I didn't want him to wake up and be horrified.

JACK: I can't believe it. This girl. She's just gone. And all I've got is the smell of her. Woodsmoke, salt, wet wool, soap. I just. It's like I've been shot. It's so humiliating. It bloody hurts.

JUNE: If I'd stayed. If I had the guts. Why didn't I? Why couldn't I keep him? Keep him alive?

BEN: He just cuts sick and wants to go home, right there and then, moment he wakes up.

WILL: We're like half asleep and he's chuckin our stuff in the car.

BEN: Down the steps, everywhere.

WILL: Callin us fifty kinds of shithead.

BEN: Piled us into the car and just fanged it.

WILL: Like he was tryin to scare us or something.
I mean, you've seen the road there, through the
forest.

JACK: Fucked everything up. Those bastards.

BEN: Man, I was brickin it. We're takin bends
on two wheels. He's doin it deliberately, like
he's gettin us to crack. Like he's tryin to force
somethin out of us.

WILL: Like what, for instance? What the fuck's he
want from us?

BEN: I don't know. Like some kind of apology,
maybe?

WILL: Nothing to apologize for.

BEN: I dunno. I feel bad.

WILL: That's a hangover, you goose.

BEN: The trees flash by. The morning light
flickering through like an epileptic fit. Want
to chuck but I'm too scared to move, the car's

sliding on the bends and he's like a maniac at the wheel. Hasn't even put a seatbelt on, I'm shitting myself.

JUNE: I can't tell him, the father. I know I killed him.

JACK: I know I'm doing something stupid. But they're afraid and I like that. The rage feels good. Believe me, it doesn't choose you; you choose it. You just let it have you. That's what I'm doing. I know it's stupid and dangerous, I know it's wrong. But I like it. I don't have the guts to stop, to get what I really want.

WILL: No shit, I think I'm gonna die. I think about grabbing the wheel, but mate, that's the movies. One side's the valley and the high side's all trees the size of fuck knows what.

BEN: I can still see it coming at me. Pink and green. Bigger every second.

WILL: Drifting. Everyone real quiet like we don't believe it's happening.

Sound of a hideous impact. BEN *and* WILL *are at the mercy of forces beyond their control. The world comes apart around them in slow motion.*

JACK: It just grew out of the ground in half a
second. It's like the very moment I see it I'm
there, in it, mixed against it, half here, there,
present, gone, panicked, calm. Out here in
the sappy bracken and that cat-pissy smell of
understorey you get beneath the karris. And you
can hear the sea like the tide of blood going out
between your ears, and there's no time to feel
sorry and stupid, no time to take the moment
back, only to feel. The ground is still shaking.
And I can hear them, every living thing. Beetles
and slaters working through the leaf litter.

BEN: Fuck, it was awful.

WILL: And he's not movin out there.

BEN: But he's saying something. I can't hear it over
the rain.

WILL: And I just wanna run. But I can't feel me
feet. And Ben's like touching the roof, the
doors, like it's not real. Coz it's all out of shape.
We're scrunched in, trapped in this thing like a
screwed-up bit of paper, like a used tissue.

BEN: Will was bawling.

WILL: Fucking liar.

JACK: There's rain falling. Falling such a long way. I watch the rain come down from beyond the trees. And just . . . feel.

Light on MARY.

MARY: Jack?

ADAM: [*off*] Chrissake, Mary, what is it?

MARY: No. Please.

ADAM: [*off*] I have to answer it. What if it's business?

MARY: Why do I keep remembering it this way, as if we were in bed, when the call actually came at 10.36 on a Tuesday morning? I wasn't even home. Neither was Adam. Both at work, of course. But it's what you've been dreading. The midnight call. You've lived it a thousand times already, trained yourself for it. It's just one long wait for the axe to fall. So when it comes.

The phone rings once.

MARY: When it comes.

The phone rings again, twice.

MARY: Then it's midnight wherever you are. And you know.

ADAM: [*off*] Mary, darling, it's me.

MARY: You know.

ADAM: [*off*] I'm in a taxi. I'll be there in five minutes. Mary?

MARY: And it – renders you a creature.

ADAM: [*off*] Love? You still with me? You there?

MARY: Something shameful, shocking, disgusting. But it's real. You recognize it, you know yourself in it and it's a kind of relief. To know you're real. You don't feel old and superfluous that moment. You feel like a girl with a swollen belly and a vein worming wild across her temple. Pushing. They tell you you're supposed to recover your self, to individuate. And it's true. You need your own life. So you inch towards it, or seize it. Of course you want it. It's expected. As if, in the wake of childbirth, you need civilizing. Schedules and peer reviews, KPIs and sales targets. That's what you need. Steely smiles, tears in the stairwell. But the sense memory lingers. Of being full. No man can give you that, no sisterly friendship, no

intellectual triumph can compete with that
sense of being filled up. Engorged sounds
gluttonous, revolting. Replete, that's the
word. Replete with your baby. You feel him
completely, he's of you, in you, he fills you
entirely. Pressing against your backbone, your
lungs, your bladder, rolling, floating, swimming
in you. At first it's just the idea of him but then
he grows, bigger, more insistent than any idea,
so big he's frightening, he owns you, possesses
you and it's terrible. Love. It's a horror. Because
there it is, waiting, the call, and when it comes
your legs give way. The world is black and red
and you bellow and writhe and press your head
against the steel to bring it on, to finish the job.
But you don't bloody die. You just writhe there
in your own slippery mess, full again, full of
nothing.

MARY *is reduced to a puddle of grief.*

BEN: Did you see her? His mum. At the funeral.

WILL: Fucksake, stop talking about the funeral.

JUNE: I wasn't invited. Why would they invite *me*?
No one knew.

BEN: It was awful. I couldn't bear it.

WILL: I didn't look. Just shut up about it.

JUNE: But I went anyway. Lurking.

BEN: I mean, it's like proper people, our kinda
people. And she's making this noise.

WILL: Leave off, willya?

BEN: I can feel me old man's hand on me arm like
a pincer. And people are embarrassed, annoyed
really, even the priest. You know, he does all the
heavy hitters' funerals. And I'm just keepin it
together and she goes down.

MARY *gives a rending groan. It goes on so long it's unbearable.*
The boys writhe in discomfort.

WILL: Enough!

JUNE: And I just want to lie there with her. On the
floor. It's like she's calving. I think of a cow in a
paddock, the way steam comes off her when she's
pushin, steam like a blanket over her, and the
moan goes up the valley through the trees.

MARY: Jack? I'm afraid, Jack, what will I do?

BEN: Horrible.

JUNE: It's awesome. A kind of fight she's havin. I wanna be like her, a hero. I'm jealous. I hate her. No one saw me.

BEN: And right at the end, when everyone's filing out, wiping their sweaty hands on their pants and thinking: Thank Christ that's over, I see her. The bushpig.

WILL: I mean, what the hell was she doing there? Hadn't been for her he'd still be alright. What right did she have? What, she drives five hours just to look at what she's done? Why didn't he just let her go, let her drift off to Antarctica? Turn into an iceberg, the fat bitch.

BEN: Man, I went cold.

WILL: She did us a favour. It was a heads-up.

BEN: Oh, bullshit. You were lawyered up by the Wednesday.

WILL: [*suddenly amused*] You ungrateful bastard.

BEN: Okay, he's my lawyer, too. But why didn't you say?

WILL: Was I conscious?

BEN: Why couldn't you tell 'em? When the fireys're cutting us out. Why? Mate, why'nt you tell 'em he's lying out there in the bush?

WILL: Shit, I dunno. First I was scared. I could smell petrol. I thought we'd get cooked alive in there, trussed up like pigs. That's all I could think. And then later I'm angry, 'cause he's nearly killed us. And then I'm in the ambulance and they've got that space blanket thing on me and I'm suddenly warm and safe, and I'm thinking: Thank fuck, thank fuck, and honest to God, no bullshit, I just forget he's out there.

BEN: What?

WILL: Jack. Fucksake, I forgot he's even out there. [*begins to weep*] I didn't remember him at all. How could I forget he's out there?

For a moment they are naked to the horror before them. They are children again.
And JACK MANSFIELD *fades from view.*

SCENE 13

The beach house the same night. ADAM *and* JUNE *at the end of her story.*

ADAM: You're one out of the box, you know.

JUNE: Yeah, the IGA box.

ADAM: I think you've got the wrong impression about us, June.

JUNE: No. I think I'm a realist.

ADAM: Those boys. If you wanted to press charges.

JUNE: No.

ADAM: I mean, we'd do everything in our power.

Lawyers, everything.

JUNE: I don't need it.

ADAM: But if you did. I mean to say you should treat us like family. What? What are you smiling at?

JUNE: Nothin.

ADAM: Maybe you can swing by now and then? Would you do that?

JUNE: Oh. I dunno. Maybe.

ADAM: Or come up to the city for a visit? Meet Mary?

JUNE: I don't think so. Actually, you know, I think I'll head off.

ADAM: Stay. Please.

JUNE: Nah, I'm off.

ADAM: Oh. Right.

JUNE: That's it.

ADAM: [*struggling to place* JUNE'*s evening of wine-tasting within her account*] But June, before you go, there's just one thing.

JUNE *hesitates.*

JUNE: Yeah?

ADAM: Nothing. Just . . . thanks. For telling me.
I feel like we owe you something.

JUNE: Nah. Nothin. Seeya.

ADAM *gets up to see her out and watches her go.*

ADAM: In the end I can't ask it, because I don't
want an answer that'll break the spell. But what's
the point of asking? Maybe it's all just bullshit,
a fantasy, every bit of her story, and she's made
it up to let herself feel better, give us something
honourable to hang onto. Lonely girl, unhappy
life. After all, she said she wanted to give us
something. What the hell. I believe her. Need to.
I just . . . choose to.

SCENE 14

The beach in golden sunlight. Sound of surf and gulls. MARY sits on a towel at the beach, barefoot in a summer dress and hat. She reads a book. Enter JACK as a boy. He's ten years old in boardshorts and a rash-vest, his nose and cheeks daubed with zinc cream, a boogie-board under his arm as he runs to her. The moment she hears him she has a towel at the ready. At stage left, JUNE assembles a shrine of her own at the foot of the karri tree.

JACK: Mum! Mum? Hey, Mum. Did you see?

MARY: Of course, darling. Did you think I'd sit here all day and not watch?

She wraps him up and dabs him dry.

JACK: I went left. All the way to the beach. I did a reo.

MARY: Like a god.

JACK: What?

MARY: Like a little golden god.

They begin to walk off and JACK *stoops to pick up a thong.*

JACK: Hey, look.

MARY: Leave it, love. It's just rubbish.

JACK: It's got barnacles on it.

They pause again.

JACK: What? What're you lookin at?

MARY: The colour of joy.

JACK: You're a nut.

MARY: I'll have you know I'm a very important
person, I have my own car space at work.

JACK: Nah, you're a nut.

MARY: Yes I am. Thank you for noticing. Jack love,
it's just a thong.

JUNE *places a single thong on the tree where the scar has congealed. She stares out to sea.*

JACK: Hey, maybe the other one will float in too.

MARY: Maybe.

Fade slowly to black.

Jack (Paul Ashcroft)

Production Notes

Shrine was first produced by the Black Swan State Theatre Company, premiering at the Heath Ledger Theatre at the State Theatre Centre of Western Australia on 31 August 2013. On 19 and 20 September 2013 it was performed at the Albany Entertainment Centre, and from 26–29 September it played at the Playhouse, Canberra Theatre Centre, as part of the Collected Works: Australia 2013 program for the Centenary of Canberra celebrations.

CAST AND CREW

Paul Ashcroft	JACK MANSFIELD
John Howard	ADAM MANSFIELD
Luke McMahon	WILL
Sarah McNeill	MARY MANSFIELD
Will McNeill	BEN
Whitney Richards	JUNE FENTON
Kate Cherry	DIRECTOR
Trent Suidgeest	SET AND LIGHTING DESIGNER
Kyle Bockmann	ASSOCIATE LIGHTING DESIGNER
Ben Collins	SOUND DESIGNER

Fiona Bruce	COSTUME DESIGNER
Emily McLean	ASSISTANT DIRECTOR
Chrissie Parrott	MOVEMENT DIRECTOR
Michael Maclean	STAGE MANAGER
Emily Stokoe	ASSISTANT STAGE MANAGER
Marie Nitschke-McGregor	WARDROBE ASSISTANT/DRESSER
Artsworkshop	SET CONSTRUCTION

June (Whitney Richards) in rehearsal

BLACK SWAN STATE THEATRE COMPANY PRESENTS

31 | 15
AUG | SEP

HEART BREAK IN
A LANDSCAPE
INHABITED BY
GHOSTS.

HEATH LEDGER
THEATRE
STATE THEATRE
CENTRE OF WA

SHRINE

BY TIM WINTON

WARNING:
Shrine contains coarse language, smoking,
atmospheric haze, male full frontal nudity and drug use

CITY *of* PERTH
WINTER ARTS SEASON

DURATION *Approx. 85 mins (no interval)*

black swan
STATE THEATRE COMPANY

  720 ABC The West Australian WorleyParsons WATER Chevron RioTinto www.bsstc.com.au

Adam (John Howard)

Mary (Sarah McNeill)

From left: Will (Luke McMahon), Ben (Will McNeill),
Jack (Paul Ashcroft) and Adam (John Howard)

From left: Ben (Will McNeill), June (Whitney Richards)
and Will (Luke McMahon)

From left: Will (Luke McMahon), Ben (Will McNeill), Jack (Paul Ashcroft)
and June (Whitney Richards)

From left: Ben (Will McNeill), Will (Luke McMahon), Jack (Paul Ashcroft), June (Whitney Richards) and Adam (John Howard)

From left: Will (Luke McMahon), Ben (Will McNeill), June (Whitney Richards) and Jack (Paul Ashcroft)

Director's Note

Shrine goes to the heart of parenthood. We love our children, we want them to fly, be fearless, daring, rise above the crowd, be the leader, take chances, and yet because we love our children we want them to be safe, fit in, take no chances, not stick their head out of the crowd, live forever, and never hurt themselves. Parenting is a delight and a terror; as a new father wrote to me once, it is like having your heart ripped open and filled with everything, love, joy, pain and terror.

Tim's ability to bring a landscape to life and reveal the psychology of the inhabitants is unique. The vast array of theatrical vocabulary we could choose to bring his work to life is testament to his extraordinary storytelling skills.

Like every contemporary playwright, Tim plays with form, and he knows his stuff, employing the direct address of Shakespeare, the static devotion to language of more formal theatre with bursts of energy, and the brilliant shifts in form, moments of expressionism, heartfelt confrontations, battles with unruly landscape that shift into surprising embrace. Tim has given us licence to play and explore characters that don't usually grace the main stage: surfers, privileged boys, underdogs, and dropouts.

In bringing this amazing array of characters to life, Tim has explored the idea of class and privilege in a society that likes to believe there is no such thing, and he has exposed our great fear. Why is it so hard to get our boys safely through being teenagers? Why is our landscape dotted with shrines to broken dreams and lost opportunities? Why is it so hard for us to talk about teenage deaths in cars without reducing terrible sorrow and grief to cliché? Tim never dictates how we view his work, but creates questions about us. He makes our fears and ambitions and desires mythological in our own landscapes.

Thank you Tim for your generosity, your grace and for your compassion for Australians from all walks of life. You can pay us no greater compliment than to give us the gift of your words. I hope you come back and play again soon.

Kate Cherry
Director

From left: Adam (John Howard), director Kate Cherry
and Will (Luke McMahon) in rehearsal

Acknowledgements

The author acknowledges reference on page 308 to 'Stay (Just a Little Bit Longer)', Maurice Williams, 1960. The quote on page 332 is from Charles Birch, *Feelings*, UNSW Press, 1995.